Geomorphic Adjustment of the Washita River
Washita Battlefield National Historic Site, Oklahoma

Natural Resource Technical Report NPS/NRPC/WRD/NRTR—2007/070

Dr. Richard A. Marston
Department of Geography
Kansas State University
Manhattan, KS 66506-2904

Dr. Todd Halihan
School of Geology
Oklahoma State University
Stillwater, OK 74078-3031

This report was prepared under Task Order 03-05 of Interagency Agreement 238099002 between the National Park Service and the U.S. Geological Survey.

December 2007

U.S. Department of the Interior
National Park Service
Natural Resource Program Center
Fort Collins, Colorado

The Natural Resource Publication series addresses natural resource topics that are of interest and applicability to a broad readership in the National Park Service and to others in the management of natural resources, including the scientific community, the public, and the NPS conservation and environmental constituencies. Manuscripts are peer-reviewed to ensure that the information is scientifically credible, technically accurate, and appropriately written for the intended audience and is designed and published in a professional manner.

The Natural Resources Technical Reports series is used to disseminate the peer-reviewed results of scientific studies in the physical, biological, and social sciences for both the advancement of science and the achievement of the National Park Service's mission. The reports provide contributors with a forum for displaying comprehensive data that are often deleted from journals because of page limitations. Current examples of such reports include the results of research that address natural resource management issues, natural resource inventory and monitoring activities, resource assessment reports, scientific literature reviews, and peer reviewed proceedings of technical workshops, conferences, or symposia.

Views, statements, findings, conclusions, recommendations, and data in this report are solely those of the author(s) and do not necessarily reflect views and policies of the U.S. Department of the Interior, NPS. Mention of trade names or commercial products does not constitute endorsement or recommendation for use by the National Park Service.

Printed copies of reports in these series may be produced in a limited quantity and they are only available as long as the supply lasts. This report is also available from the Water Resources Division website (http://www.nature.nps.gov/water/wrdpub.cfm) on the internet, or by sending a request to the address on the back cover.

Please cite this publication as:

Marston, R. A., and T. Halihan. 2007. Geomorphic adjustment of the Washita River, Washita Battlefield National Historic Site, Oklahoma. Natural Resource Technical Report NPS/NRPC/WRD/NRTR—2007/070. National Park Service, Fort Collins, Colorado.

NPS D-44A, December 2007

Contents

Figures

Tables

Appendixes

Acknowledgments

We wish to express our appreciation to the Joel Wagner, Wetland Program Leader of the National Park Service, Water Resources Division, for funding this project. David "Chip" Leslie, Unit Leader of the Oklahoma Cooperative Fish and Wildlife Research Unit, provided the funding conduit and administrative support necessary to undertake this project on the Oklahoma State University campus. The Principal Investigators wish to acknowledge the critical assistance in data acquisition and analysis provided by Dan Wisleder, whose M.S. thesis in Geography at OSU was supported by this project. Outstanding field assistance was also provided by OSU Geology undergraduates Chris Ennen and Brandon Binford. An initial draft of this report was improved by addressing thoughtful review comments by the NPS Water Resources Division. Any errors or omissions that remain may be attributed to the authors.

Dr. Richard A. Marston, Kansas State University
Dr. Todd Halihan, Oklahoma State University

1. Introduction

The Washita Battlefield National Historic Site (WBNHS) preserves and commemorates the site of the Southern Cheyenne village of Peace Chief Black Kettle that was attacked by the 7th U.S. Cavalry under Lt. Col. George A. Custer just before dawn on November 27, 1868. The battlefield is a floodplain of sandy loam soils through which the Washita River meanders as a single-thread, low-gradient channel. The present channel and the fringe of the floodplain are lined by trees and shrubs, many of which are non-native species.

A full description of the hydrologic environment and significant water-resource issues of the WBNHS is presented in Reber et al. (1999). This report notes the key impact of upstream flood control dams but notes that "The local impacts of altered flow conditions upon stream channel morphology… and adjacent riparian zones are largely unknown." Inglis and Wagner performed a reconnaissance survey of the WBNHS in 2001 and concluded that a two-phase study of watershed hydrology and fluvial geomorphology was warranted. Focus should be placed on "…determining the channel form that would be stable and would support a properly functioning riparian ecosystem under current and anticipated future watershed conditions. A historic vegetation survey and current species inventory of the WBNHS were undertaken by Hoagland et al. (2005) for the National Park Service. They alerted the NPS to the possibility of rapid change to the riparian ecosystem by invasive species.

2. Objectives

The objectives of this project were to:

1) evaluate the present geomorphic condition of the Washita River through the Battlefield;

2) evaluate the adjustment of the present channel to the prevailing water and sediment supply to the channel, and how this adjustment has changed through time;

3) evaluate the likelihood that a modified channel similar to that which existed in 1868 could remain in equilibrium with the present conditions of flow and sediment; and

4) based on the findings of this study, develop conceptual alternatives for achieving a stable channel form and functional riparian system along distinct reaches of the river that are as close to the historic conditions as possible.

3. Study Area

The Washita River is a tributary of the Red River. The river begins in the northeast panhandle of Texas and flows into western Oklahoma. The river flows 50 miles from its source before it enters the WBNHS immediately upstream of Cheyenne, Oklahoma (Figures 1-2). The WBNHS has been in private hands since the 1890s, not having been claimed by descendants of the 1868 battle. The site was farmed until 2001.

The Washita River watershed is situated in the High Plains and Western Redbed Plains geomorphic province. This region is characterized by gently rolling hills on flat-lying Permian sandstone and shale. Annual precipitation is 686 mm (27 in.). Present land use is rangeland with some irrigated cropland.

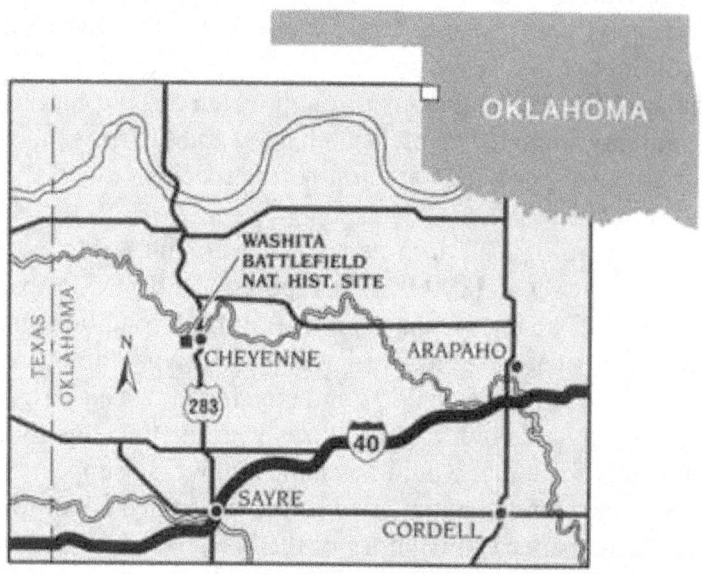

Figure 1. Location of the WBNHS.

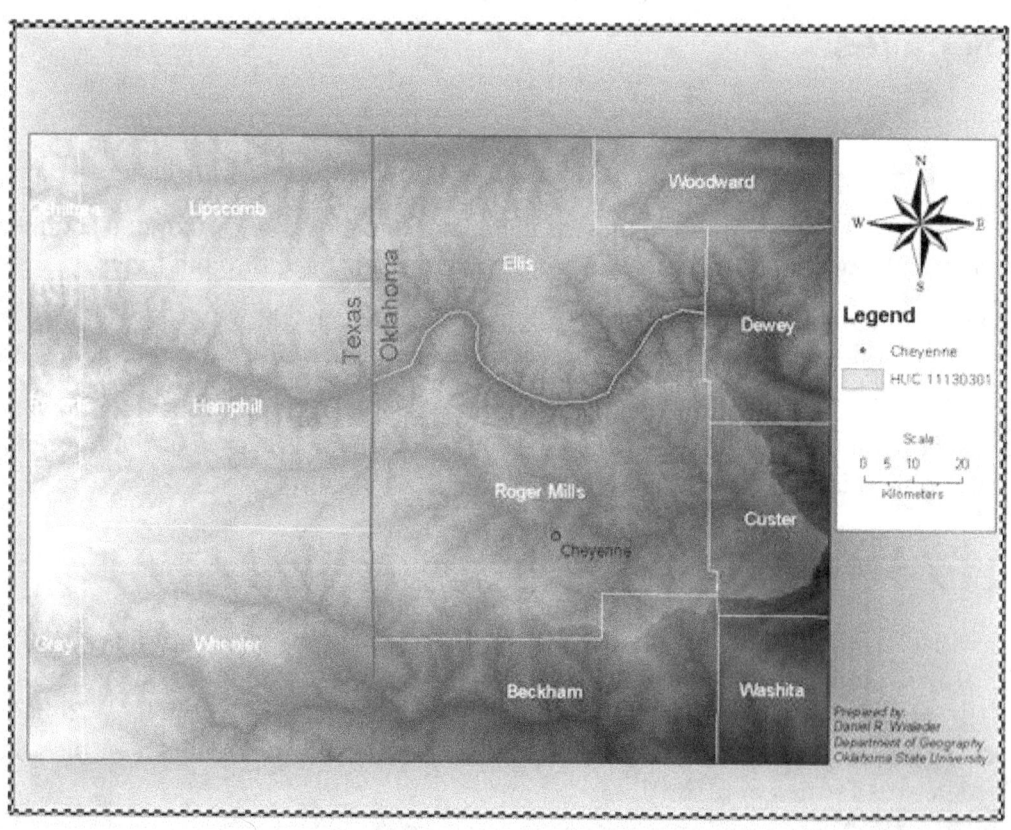

Figure 2. Position of WBNHS (Cheyenne, OK) within the Washita River watershed.

4. Methods

4.1 Methods for Objective #1: Present-Day Channel

Objective #1 was achieved by completing several tasks:

1) Channel cross-sections were measured at 36 different locations, roughly spaced at 30-meter intervals along the channel. Each cross-section was located with a GPS and with measurements using standard survey techniques (Platts et al. 1987). Morphological features measured included: channel cross-section shape, channel unit type, and substrate.

2) Two nested sets of piezometers were established—one near the upstream reach of the river within the WBNHS and one near the downstream reach. The piezometers were equipped with data loggers so changes in stream flow could be related to fluctuations in the alluvial water table. It was critical to determine if the stream was tied to the alluvial water table and, if so, for what portion of the year. The alluvial water table affects the viability of riparian species that might be chosen for channel restoration purposes. Piezometers were installed with a Geoprobe owned by the Oklahoma State University School of Geology.

3) Subsurface investigations were conducted using sediment core data, electrical resistivity imaging data, monitoring wells, and external data sources.

4) For each reach, conclusions were formulated on the relative stability of the present channel, including the ability to contain flood flows, the ability to form and maintain point bars, and the likelihood of future avulsions, meander shifts, downcutting or aggradation. Formulated conclusions as to whether the present channel in each reach is still in transition or has adjusted to the present water and sediment regime, a decision that can be confounded by many factors (Schumm 1991).

4.2 Methods for Objective #2: Channel Adjustment over Time

Objective #2 was achieved by completing the following tasks:

5) Streamflow records were analyzed for the gaging station on the Washita River at Cheyenne, located approximately 8 km (5 miles) downstream of the WBNHS.

6) Described and explained the effect of construction of reservoirs on tributaries of the Washita River upstream of the WBNHS.

7) Described plan view and, to the extent possible, cross-section changes in the Washita River over the period covered by large-scale aerial photos. Created channel maps from digitized aerial photos of the Washita River in the WBNIIS (as per Graf 1984), which were available for the following years:

> 1936 (National Archives, B&W, 1:20,000)
> 1961 (ASCS, B&W, 1:20,000)
> 1966 (NASA, B&W, 1:40,000)

3

1974 (ASCS, B&W, 1:40,000)
1982 (USFS, color, 1:24,000)
1996 (USGS, B&W, 1:40,000)

8) Conducted a literature review of sources that describes historical changes in the channel.

9) Conducted shallow resistivity surveys to detect former locations of the Washita River channel.

4.3 Methods for Objective #3: 1868 Channel vs. Present-Day Conditions

Objective #3 was achieved by completing the following tasks:

10) Using historical records, described the geomorphology of the Washita River as it existed at the time of the battle in November 1868. Foremost among these accounts was the work by Lees et al. (1997), historical photos (e.g., an 1890 photo of the channel by H.L. Scott), and maps (e.g., an 1873 map by the General Lands Office Survey).

11) Compared the present form-process adjustments to those that would have had to exist in a channel of the type that existed in 1868.

4.4 Methods for Objective #4: Alternatives for a Stable Modern-Day Channel

Objective #4 was achieved by synthesizing findings from the first 10 tasks:

12) Evaluated the likelihood that a modified channel similar to that which existed in 1868 could remain in equilibrium with the present conditions of flow and sediment.

13) Based on the findings of this study, developed conceptual alternatives for achieving a stable channel form and functional riparian system along distinct reaches of the river that are as close to the historic conditions as possible.

5. Results

5.1 Results for Objective #1: Present-Day Channel

In 16-19 July 2001, National Park Service Water Resource Division employees Richard Inglis (Hydrologist) and Joel Wagner (Wetlands Program Leader) conducted a survey of the stream channel and riparian vegetation along the Washita River in the WBNHS (Inglis and Wagner 2001). They evaluated the "functioning condition" of the channel and riparian zone (Table 1). Stream/riparian areas are said to be "functioning properly" when adequate vegetation, landform, or large woody debris is present to:

1) dissipate stream energy associated with high water flows, thereby reducing erosion and improving water quality;

2) filter sediment, capture bedload, and aid floodplain development;

3) improve floodwater retention and groundwater recharge;

4) develop root masses that stabilize stream banks against cutting action;

5) develop diverse ponding and channel characteristics to provide habitat and the water depths, durations, temperature regimes, and substrates necessary for fish populations, waterfowl breeding, and other uses; and

6) support greater biodiversity.

If channel reaches are not in a proper functioning condition (PFC), they are rated as either "functional-at-risk" or "non-functional."

Inglis and Wagner divided the Washita River within the WBNHS into four reaches, labeled 1-4 from west to east. The cross-sections surveyed in the present study were divided into the same four reaches, with additional data acquired for three cross-sections upstream of the WBNHS and three cross-sections downstream of the WBNHS. Data were collected for 35 cross-sections: three upstream of the WBNHS (yellow in Figure 3), six in Reach # 1 (red in Figure 3), six in Reach #2 (blue in Figure 3), six in Reach # 3 (green in Figure 3), 11 in Reach # 4 (pink in Figure 3), and three downstream of the WBNHS (not shown in Figure 3; off the right edge of the aerial photo).

The following descriptions of reaches (Sections 5.11, 5.12 and 5.13 below) are quoted directly from Inglis and Wagner (2001):

5.1.1 Reaches #1 and #3

"These two river reaches were very similar and were treated together for this assessment. They are characterized by virtually straight channels with steep channel banks on both sides (typically 4-5 feet in height) and no sign of point bar development or sinuosity that would be expected for this stream. Flows that overtopped the channel in the recent past

5

have deposited sand immediately adjacent to the banks, creating small levees that are being colonized by upland vegetation. For the most part, the channel and associated features are not of the form that would be expected in this geomorphic setting. The channel has a high width/depth ratio with very uniform depths, which we judged to be out of balance with present watershed characteristics. The channel bed was typically 8-10 feet wide and was composed of predominantly fine sand. Coarse woody debris was almost non-existent, so there was no contribution from that source to a diversity of channel structure or dissipation of flood flow energy.

As a result of the poor geomorphic condition, the riparian vegetation was also in poor shape. There is substantial invasion of the floodplain by upland species such as black locust (*Robinea pseudoacacia*), giant sand reed grass (*Calamovilfa gigantean*), cheatgrass (*Bromus tectorum*) as well as Tamarisk (*Tamarix* sp.). However, tamarisk appears to be in decline due to park eradication efforts and an apparent insect infestation. Black willow is fairly well represented on the floodplain in at least two age classes, but there has been virtually no recruitment of cottonwoods (*Populus deltoides*) for many years due to the lack of point bar development and the apparent lack of seed sources from mature trees. Due to the high, steep channel banks, there is a clear lack of stream bank vegetation of the type that would protect against erosion under high flows (e.g., bulrush, spike rush, sedges, willows, cottonwoods).

We rated these streams as 'non-functional' based on the lack of appropriate geomorphic and vegetative features that provide the erosion control, habitat structure, and other beneficial characteristics listed under the PFC definition above."

5.1.2 Reach #2

"This stream reach was in better shape than reaches 1 and 3 in terms of developing sinuosity, width/depth ratios, and pool-riffle channel characteristics that are more in balance with the landscape setting. Point bars are forming and retain sufficient moisture to support bank and channel stabilizing herbaceous vegetation such as American bulrush (*Scirpus americanus*) and common three-square (*Scirpus pungens*). However, cover is not yet adequate to protect these areas from erosion during higher flow events. Willows were observed in a variety of age classes along the banks and upper point bar locations, including 1-2 year old plants. Although the point bars are also suitable for cottonwood recruitment, young plants were encountered only occasionally. We suspect that this is due more to the lack of nearby cottonwood seed sources than to a lack of suitable locations for seedling germination and establishment.

Although the above trends are mostly good signs of stream and riparian zone recovery from past perturbations, this reach is still experiencing significant stream bank erosion in many areas (active erosion is evident on approximately 50% of the stream reach). Lack of large woody debris and bank stabilizing riparian tree root systems (both associated with the lack of mature cottonwoods and willows along the banks) have continued to make this reach susceptible to significant erosion under high stream flow events.

Table 1. Properly functioning condition (PFC) of stream/riparian systems (Inglis and Wagner 2001).

	Factor	Reaches #1 & #3	Reach #2	Reach #4
Hydrology				
1	Floodplain above bankfull is inundated in "relatively frequent" events	Yes	Yes	Yes
2	Where beaver dams are present they are active and stable	n/a	n/a	n/a
3	Sinuosity, width/depth ratio, and gradient are in balance with the landscape setting	**No**	Yes	Yes
4	Riparian-wetland area is widening or has achieved potential extent	**No**	Yes	Yes
5	Upland watershed is not contributing to riparian-wetland degradation	Yes	Yes	Yes
Vegetation				
6	Diverse age-class distribution exists for riparian-wetland vegetation	Yes	**No**	Yes
7	Diverse composition exists for riparian-wetland vegetation (for maintenance/recovery)	Yes	Yes	Yes
8	Species present indicate maintenance of riparian-wetland soil moisture characteristics	**No**	Yes	Yes
9	Streambank vegetation is comprised of those plants that have root masses capable of withstanding high streamflow events	No	No	No
10	Riparian-wetland plants exhibit high vigor	Yes	Yes	Yes
11	Adequate riparian-wetland vegetative cover is present to protect banks and dissipate energy during high flows	Yes	**No**	Yes
12	Plants communities are an adequate source of coarse and/or large woody material (for maintenance & recovery)	No	No	No
Erosion/Deposition				
13	Floodplain and channel characteristics (e.g., rocks, overflow channels, large woody debris) are adequate to dissipate energy	No	No	No
14	Point bars are revegetating with riparian-wetland vegetation	n/a	Yes	Yes
15	Lateral stream movement is associated with natural sinuosity	**No**	Yes	Yes
16	System is vertically stable	Yes	Yes	Yes
17	Stream is in balance with the water and sediment being supplied by the watershed (i.e., no excessive erosion or deposition	Yes	**No**	Yes

Figure 3. Location of cross-sections surveyed in this study (Base photo from U.S. Department of Agriculture, 1999). Reach numbers correspond with those described by Inglis and Wagner (2001).

The lack of large woody debris, limited cover of native herbaceous stream bank vegetation, continued excessive bank erosion, and susceptibility to continued erosion under higher stream flows led us to rate this stream reach as "non-functional." Even a single high flow event has the potential to negate much of the recovery that has occurred in this reach."

5.1.3 Reach #4

"Of the four reaches we evaluated, reach 4 was in the best functional condition. Sinuosity, width-depth ratios, and pool-riffle channel characteristics appear to be appropriate to the landscape setting. Point bars are present and are becoming vegetated with appropriate herbaceous and woody species. Herbaceous cover and willow establishment along stream banks and on point bars was greater than in other reaches and appears to be on an upward trend. We observed significantly more cottonwood recruitment in this reach, which we believe is due to both the presence of appropriate geomorphology and the proximity to mature cottonwood trees (seed sources). A problem for most of this reach is the shortage of large woody debris and tree root systems necessary to dissipate flood energy, protect banks from erosion, and create channel

8

habitat diversity. Older cottonwoods are too far from the river to provide such benefits and have not been replaced except for young saplings in a few places. Another problem in this reach is that in some areas farming activities reach to the stream bank with no riparian buffer. A buffer zone of riparian vegetation is needed in these areas to protect against sediment deposition from farm fields, to provide tree cover for stream temperature control, and to provide large woody debris and tree roots as described previously.

This reach is functional in terms of most of the hydrologic, vegetative, and erosion/deposition factors we evaluated. However, we rated it 'functional-at risk' due to insufficient large woody debris, which leaves the area susceptible to erosion in large flood events that could eliminate much of the recovery seen in the reach to date. We also characterized the overall trend of this reach as 'upward.' This means that over time (and in the absence of extreme flows in the near term) we expect that the young cottonwoods and willows here will continue to mature and will begin to provide the missing woody debris and tree root elements that put this reach at risk."

5.1.4 Cross-Section Data from Current Study

The substrate data for cross-sections, stratified by the reaches designated by Inglis and Wagner (2001), are presented in Table 2. The corresponding channel cross-section profiles are given in Appendix A. The percent clay is higher in Reach #1 and Reach #3 than in Reach #2 or Reach #4. This is consistent with the observation by Inglis and Wagner (2001), matched in this study, that banks are higher and more vertical in Reaches #1 and #3 than in Reaches #2 and #4. Channels in Reaches #1 and #3 are more narrow and deep than those in Reaches #2 and #4. Channels are expected to be more narrow and deep as the percent silt-clay in banks increases.

5.1.5 Subsurface Investigations of WBNHS

The investigation of the subsurface properties of the WBNHS was designed to answer three specific questions. First, does the subsurface distribution of sediment on the site provide any insight into the structure and location of the site during the time of the battle? Secondly, what is the current relationship between the Washita River and the ground water on the site? Finally, does this relationship appear to have changed since 1868?

In order to address these questions, four primary data sources were utilized. Sediment core samples were collected to determine sediment properties at two locations in the battlefield. Electrical resistivity imaging (ERI) was performed at six sites across the battlefield to evaluate the sediment structure across larger portions of the site. Monitoring wells were installed at the site to monitor the relationship between ground water and the water level in the Washita River. This was combined with U.S. Geological Survey stream data and precipitation data collected for the area to understand the local ground water system.

9

Table 2. Cross-section data collected in the present study. See Appendix A for cross-section profiles.

Reach	Cross Section	Channel Unit Type	Clay (%) < .0039 mm	Silt (%) 0.0039 to 0.6mm	Sand (%) 0.6 to 2 mm	Gravel (%) (2 to 64 mm	Cobble (%) 0.64 to 256 mm	Boulder (%) > 256 mm	Bedrock (%)
u/s of WBNHS	1	glides	0	0	85	15	0	0	0
u/s of WBNHS	2	glides	0	0	95	5	0	0	0
u/s of WBNHS	3	riffles	0	0	100	0	0	0	0
1	1	glides	10	0	85	5	0	0	0
1	2	glides	0	0	99	1	0	0	0
1	3	riffles	40	0	60	0	0	0	0
1	4	riffles	0	0	98	2	0	0	0
1	5	riffles	50	0	50	0	0	0	0
1	6	riffles	20	0	80	0	0	0	0
2	1	riffles	20	0	80	0	0	0	0
2	2	riffles							
2	4	riffles	0	10	80	10	0	0	0
2	3	riffles	0	0	100	0	0	0	0
2	2a	riffles	10	0	90	0	0	0	0
2	1a	riffles	40	60 %	0	0	0	0	0
3	1	riffles	17	0	80	3	0	0	0
3	2	riffles	10	0	90	0	0	0	0
3	3	riffles	10	0	90	0	0	0	0
3	4	riffles	60	0	40	0	0	0	0
3	5	pool	0	0	100	0	0	0	0
3	6	glides	0	0	100	0	0	0	0
4	1	glides	0	0	100	0	0	0	0
4	2	riffles	0	0	98	2	0	0	0
4	3	riffles	2	0	98	0	0	0	0
4	4	riffles	5	0	95	0	0	0	0
4	5	riffles	10	0	90	0	0	0	0
4	6	riffles	10	0	90	0	0	0	0
4	7	riffles	20	0	80	0	0	0	0
4	8	riffles	15	0	85	0	0	0	0
4	9	riffles	15	0	80	5	0	0	0
4	10	riffles	10	0	80	10	0	0	0
4	11	riffles	40	0	60	0	0	0	0
d/s of WBNHS	1	riffles	0	0	100	0	0	0	0
d/s of WBNHS	2	riffles	0	0	95	0	5	0	0
d/s of WBNHS	3	riffles	0	0	100	0	0	0	0

5.1.5.a Sediment Core Data

Two sediment cores, MW 1 and MW 9, were collected during the installation of the monitoring wells on the site (Figure 5). These cores were used as a calibration for the ERI images collected on the site and to determine the grain size for evaluating the likelihood that cottonwood trees could exist over different areas of the site. The 1.5 inch cores were collected using a direct push dual tube sampling technique in 4-foot increments. One core was collected from each well site on the far east and far west portion of the site.

These cores were analyzed to determine grain size using a Coulter LS 230 Particle Size Analyzer. The procedure used for particle size analysis is as follows:

1) Put ~0.5 gram of sample in plastic bottle. Add ~20 mL of sodium meta-phosphate, {Na-mPO4 [1g/1L]}.

2) Sonicate for ten minutes.

3) Shake vigorously.

4) Add sample mixture until PID is 45%-55% (usually a few mL solution is adequate).

5) Run new sample twice.

6) Compare results of two tests for QC.

7) Clean Coulter instrument.

8) Repeat with next sample.

The instrument provided good repeatability and allowed a detailed analysis of the two cores that were sampled on the site.

The particle size analyzer technique provided good repeatability for the core samples (Figure 4). The core from the west side of the site, WB-01, was predominantly silt. A small clay layer and a fine sand layer were present, but the core was dominantly medium silt. The east side of the site had obvious sand exposed at the surface. The sand extended 15 feet into the subsurface until it reached a silt layer. The core became sandier again at depth, but finer sand than at the surface.

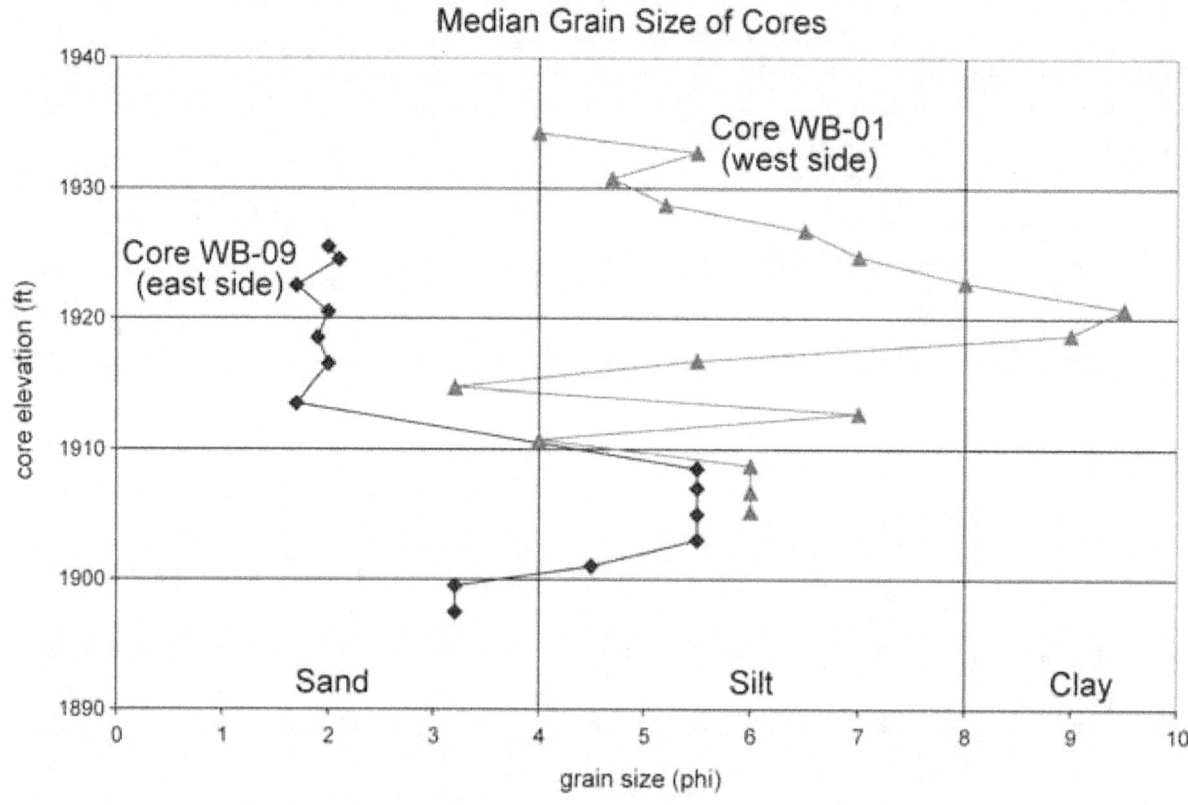

Figure 4. Median grain size for two cores collected from site. A wide range of grain sizes exist on the site, but the site is dominated by silt with sandy areas and limited clay lenses.

5.1.5.b Electrical Resistivity Imaging Data

ERI is a geophysical technique that can provide two- or three-dimensional images (pictures) of the subsurface that provide a more complete understanding of the distribution of sediment at the battlefield site. ERI provides detailed data on the subsurface electrical properties of the location where the data is collected. For this site, it is expected that finer grained materials will be more conductive than coarser grain materials. Some other physical influences on the electrical properties of the subsurface include variations in salinity and contaminants that are located on the site. Neither of these effects is expected at the battlefield site.

The first phase of ERI data collection occurred during June 2004. This data was collected to coincide with the locations of the wells and sediment coring locations (Figure 5 and Appendix C). The results were promising for providing a method to locate older channel deposits and were subsequently deployed during May 2005 to sample the area of the park where the 1868 channel was expected to exist.

Figure 5. Map of subsurface investigations of WBNHS. Aerial photo is one meter resolution image collected on 10/1/2003 and downloaded from terraserver.com.

13

Electrical resistivity imaging of the site was useful in delineating the areas of sand and silt across the site due to the conductive nature of the battlefield (Appendix C). The results are described first in terms of the electrical properties, then in terms of the relationship with grain size. The datasets provided by this method only measure the electrical properties of the soil, but have been demonstrated to be drillable in correlating to various geological parameters.

The ERI datasets ranged from 1-1000 ohm-meters for the site, but the vast majority of the datasets occurred in the range from 4-40 ohm-meters. The shallow areas of the images were conductive in areas of silty soils (<14 ohm-meters), and resistive (>24 ohm-meters) in sandy soils. The surface correlation seems to indicate that more resistive areas near the surface are sandier deposits. The middle portions of the images are dominantly conductive materials. This would be expected to be silty materials. Only one image (Figure C5) shows a resistive body in this portion of the image. This portion of the image was cored and demonstrated to be a sandy region. This provides the only indication of any buried channels at depth. The remainder of the images suggests that sandy deposits are geologically recent phenomena for the site.

The deeper portions of the images become more resistive at a depth of approximately 20-40 feet. These deeper portions of the images were not sampled by coring. Since much of the area surrounding the park has bedrock outcropping at the surface, it is expected that the undulating resistive surface at depth is the presence of bedrock beneath the site. The variations in the surface are suggestive of channels in some areas of the images, but they would be filled with silt size material.

The core data combined with the ERI data indicate the site is dominated by silt materials overlying the bedrock of the area. The sandy deposits at the surface only extend 10-15 feet deep in the areas where they exist in the images. If the sandy deposits are interpreted as geologically recent channel deposits, several candidates for 1868 channels exist in the area sampled with ERI during 2005. The methods utilized here cannot distinguish the relative or absolute ages of these channels to determine which location is the correct location of the 1868 channel.

5.1.5.c Monitoring Wells

Ten monitoring wells were installed at the site using direct push installation techniques. Two well sites were established, one on the west side of the site (south of the river) and one on the east side of the site (north of the river) (Figure 5, Table 3). Transducers (Figure 7) were installed in six wells (Wells #1, 2, 5, 6, 7, and 8) to monitor the water level over time. To assure data quality, water levels were checked with a tape measure when the data loggers were downloaded.

The monitoring wells were 1.5 inch diameter wells installed using 3.25 inch direct push borings (Figure 6). Two depths were monitored, a deep installation screened at 26-31 feet below ground surface (bgs), and a shallow depth screened at 11-16 feet bgs. The wells were pre-packed screens from Geophone in Salina, KS. Two surface completions were used after discussions with park staff. Four wells were completed with square riser pipes that are visible, but lockable (Figure 6). The remaining wells were completed at the ground surface (Figure 8).

Table 3. Well construction and survey data for monitoring wells at WBNHS. GPS location uses WGS 84 datum.

1.5 Inch Direct Push PVC Well Construction Design

Well Number	TMO (ft)	ToC (ft)	ToM (ft)	Screened Interval (ft)	Latitude (UTM)	Longitude (UTM)	Latitude (dd)	Longitude (dd)
WB 01	1940.00	1940.35	1940.57	26-31	14S 0435459	3942083	35.620416	-99.712694
WB 02	1940.11	1940.37	1940.11	16-11	14S 0435459	3942083	35.620416	-99.712694
WB 03		1937.23	1937.43	26-31	14S 0435488	3942066	35.620277	-99.712388
WB 04		1937.10	1937.44	16-11	14S 0435488	3942066	35.620277	-99.712388
WB 05		1937.14	1937.31	26-31	14S 0453457	3942050	35.621138	-99.513972
WB 06		1937.11	1937.29	16-11	14S 0453457	3942050	35.621138	-99.513972
WB 07		1929.38	1929.74	26-31	14S 0436965	3942532	35.624555	-99.696111
WB 08		1929.36	1929.68	16-11	14S 0436966	3942531	35.624555	-99.696083
WB 09		1927.10	1927.42	30-35	14S 0436996	3942530	35.624555	-99.695777
WB 10		1927.13	1927.44	14-19	14S 0436995	3942531	35.624555	-99.695777

Constructed with Square Protective Steel Risers:
WB 01
WB 02
WB 07
WB 08

Constructed with Cast Iron Manhole Flush Mounts:
WB 03
WB 04
WB 05
WB 06
WB 09
WB 10

Top of Metal Cap (ToM)

Top of Metal Opening (TMO)

Top of PVC casing (ToC)

Top of Metal Cap (ToM)

Ground

casing (ToC)

Legend

TMO:	Top Metal Opening
ToC:	Top of Casing
ToM:	Top of Metal Cap

15

The monitoring wells were useful in delineating the flow of the ground water system at the battlefield. The water levels at two depths allowed an analysis of the flow in three dimensions at the site. The wells on the west side of the battlefield proved more useful as the installation and monitoring of the west side was much simpler.

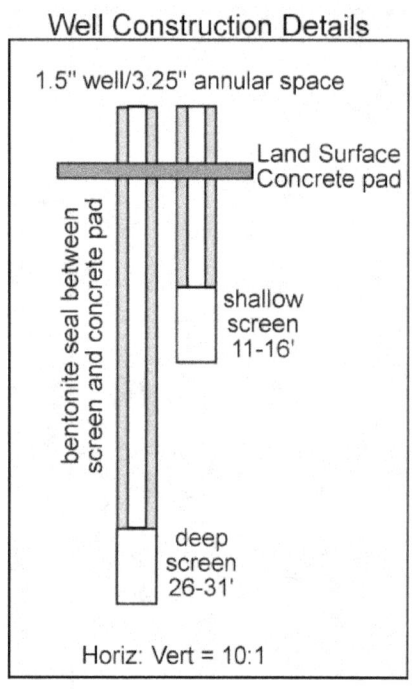

Figure 6. Well construction for monitoring wells at WBNHS. Screen depths were based on construction requirements and sufficient distance to obtain a vertical hydraulic gradient, not on knowledge of aquifer structure.

The difficulties with the east side of the site were due to several causes. The site north of the stream channel was only accessible for the direct push rig by crossing other land owner properties. The dirt roads ended several hundred yards from the well site. As this site was significantly sandier on the north side of the river, the rig became stuck several times and only two well pairs were installed. Monitoring was conducted by crossing the stream to the site on foot, but during high flow periods, this was prohibitive.

The water level in the wells varied approximately 5 feet during the study period. The water level in both the shallow and the deep wells never went below the base of the stream (Appendix B). The wells responded with the stream discharge.

If we examine the vertical hydraulic gradient for both sites, the dominant gradient is upward from the deeper portions of the aquifer to the shallower portions (Figure 9). The gradients range from 0 – 0.17 ft/ft downward and 0 – 0.027 ft/ft upward. Only Wells 3 and 4 demonstrated a downward gradient from the shallow to the deeper portions during the normal periods. During the high flow period monitored, Wells 5 and 6 indicated that downward flow was occurring during that time along with Wells 3 and 4 with the high downward gradient of 0.17 occurring between Wells 5 and 6. The normal downward gradient generally did not exceed 0.011 ft/ft. Even during the high flow event, Wells 1 and 2 still maintained an upward vertical gradient. In general, higher upward gradients correspond to higher discharge in the Washita River.

Figure 7. Photo of Wells WB-07 and WB-08, showing standpipe completion and transducer installation (2003).

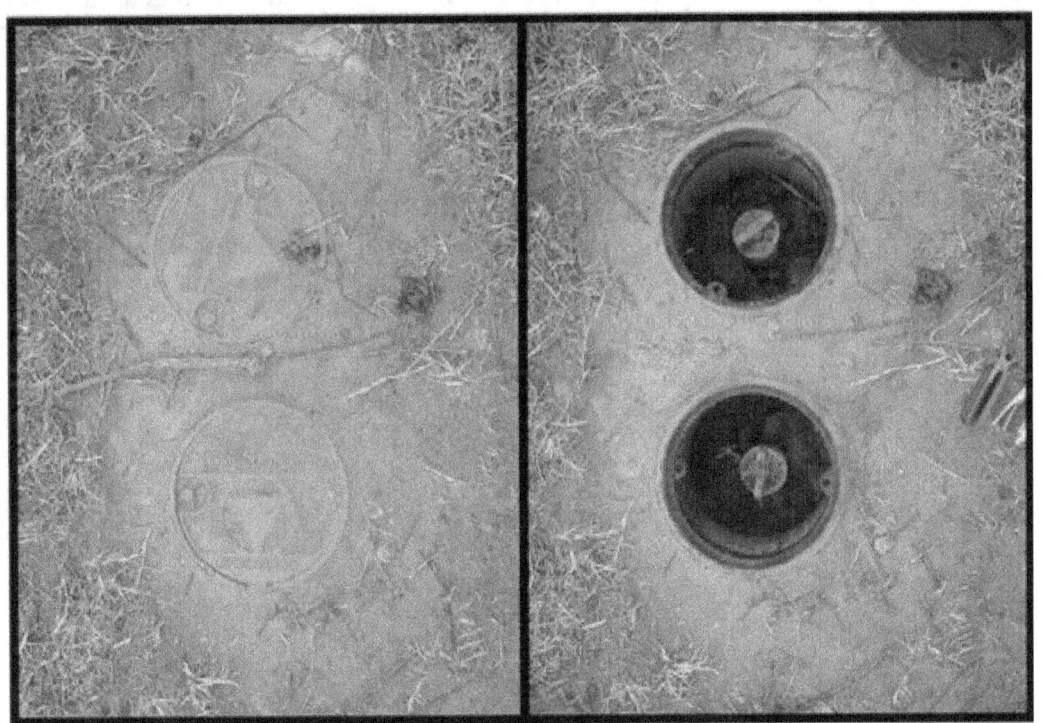

Figure 8. Photo of Wells WB-09 and WB-10 showing ground-level completion well caps used to protect PVC wells (2003).

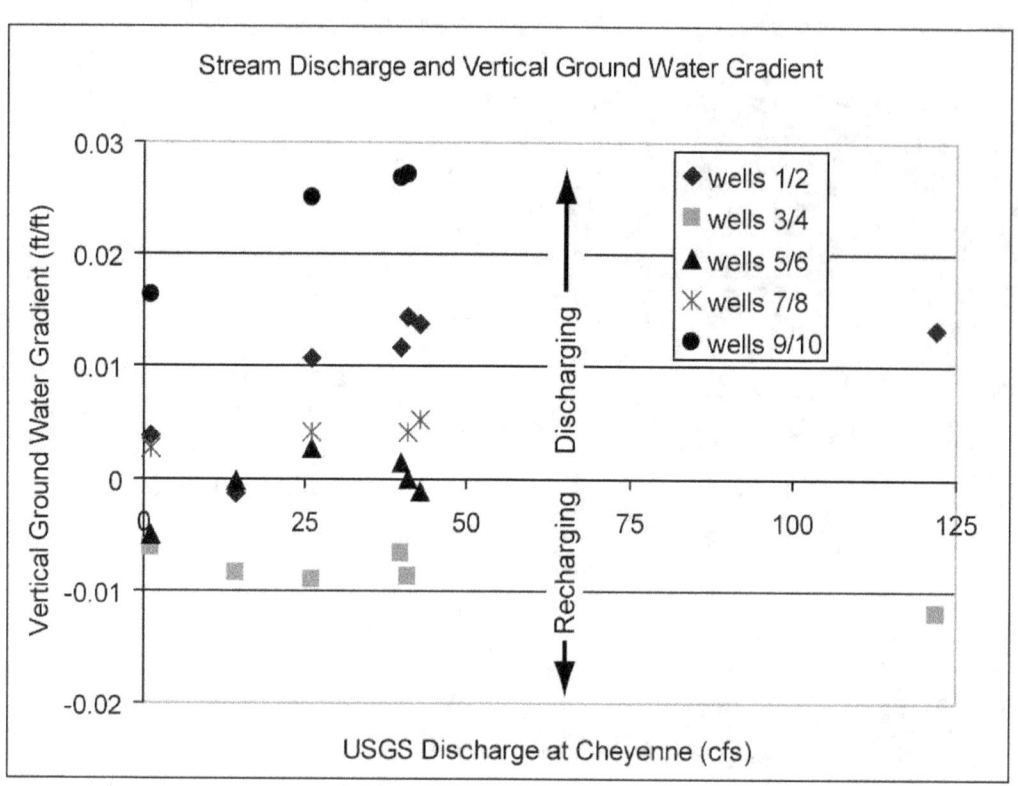

Figure 9. Vertical ground water gradient at the WBNHS compared to stream discharge.

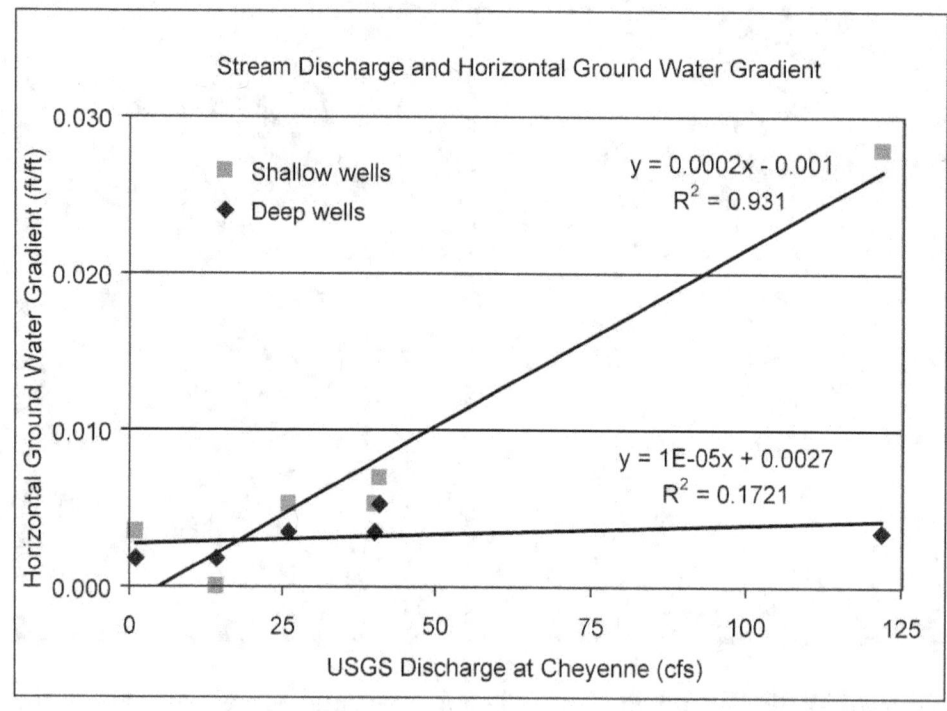

Figure 10. Horizontal ground water gradient at the WBNHS compared to stream discharge.

A former irrigation well exists to the east of Wells 3 and 4. If the well casing is leaking in the former well, it could be providing the vertical gradient observed in Wells 3 and 4. Otherwise, the remainder of the site data indicates a discharging ground water system that may recharge during significant stream discharge events.

The horizontal gradient for the west well field indicates the shallow system is more strongly connected to the stream channel than the deeper system, as expected (Figure 10).
During most time periods, the hydraulic head in the wells was higher than the stream and ground water was discharging into the river. During a single monitored high flow event, water recharged the shallow ground water system. As the ground water gradient decreased, so did the stream discharge with a nearly flat water table occurring during low flow periods. The water table appeared to start flowing down valley parallel to the stream during extreme low flow events. The relationship between the horizontal gradient and the stream discharge is much weaker for the deeper wells on the site. The orientation of the gradient was similar for both the shallow and deeper wells (Figure 11). The shallow ground water system flowed orthogonal to the Washita River with the horizontal gradient proportional to the discharge of the river. The gradient of the shallow wells ranged from nearly 0.0 to 0.028 ft/ft. The normal gradient for the site ranges from 0.003-0.005. The general flow direction ranges from 340-20 degrees, depending on the gradient. During a single low flow event, the gradient was calculated as heading east, but this may also be due to measurement error with little difference occurring between the wells.

The deeper wells had a similar orientation as the shallow wells, but during extreme highs and lows would tend to have a gradient towards the west to northwest. During normal periods, the gradient was from 0 – 30 degrees with a magnitude of 0.0017 – 0.0052 ft/ft.

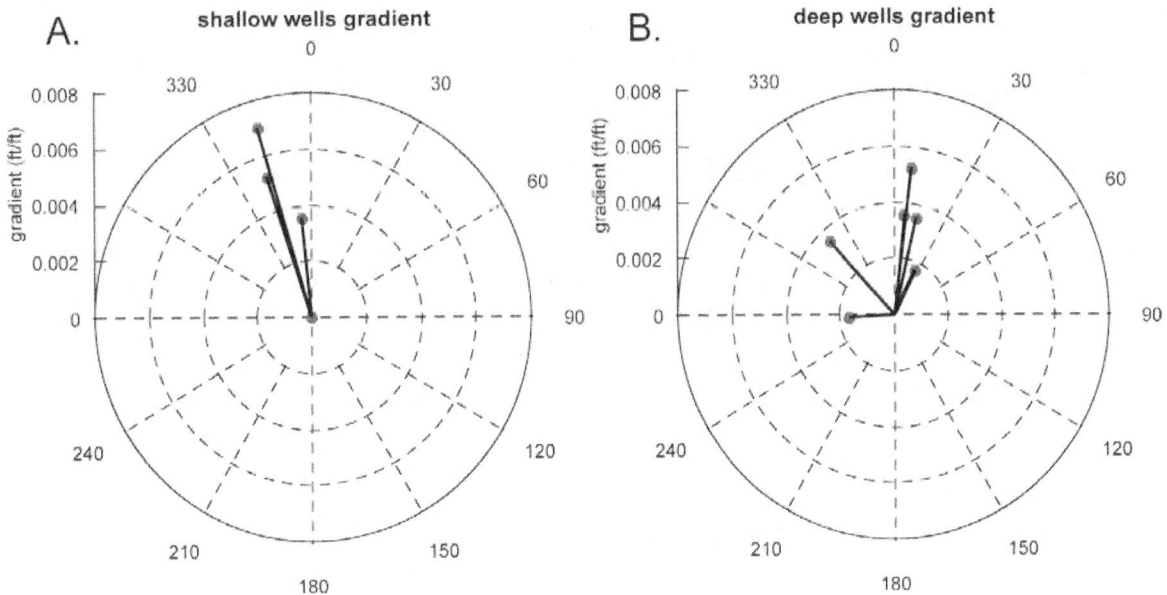

Figure 11. Direction and magnitude of the horizontal hydraulic gradient for the west well site at WBNHS. A high gradient value of 0.028 is left off of the shallow well plot for the high flow event as it is well off scale for the two plots. The dip direction for the high gradient value is 16 degrees.

5.1.5.d External Data Sources

Precipitation data was available for Cheyenne, OK, through the Mesonet data network. The precipitation record is only presented for the time of the study. Discharge data from the U.S. Geological Survey was available for stream gauging station 07316500 located on the Washita River near Cheyenne. The gauge provides data since 1937, but for comparison with the ground water record for this study, only the data for the study period is presented.

The sediment cores and ERI data provided a useful look at the subsurface structure of the site to understand the geologic variability in the subsurface. The monitoring wells and other hydrologic data provided enough data to understand the basic functioning of the ground water system. Both the geologic and hydrogeologic data provided insight into 1868 conditions at the site.

The stream discharge of the Washita River appears more strongly influence by the response of the ground water system than simple precipitation (Figures 12, 13 and 14). The precipitation does not influence the stream in direct correlation with storm events, but the stream discharge is well correlated with ground water elevation in the area.

5.1.6 Discussion

Using the subsurface data that has been collected provides insight into the questions that are of interest for the site. The subsurface distribution of sediment on the site provides insight into the structure and location of the site during the time of the battle. The lack of evidence of deeper sandy deposits indicates the distributions of sandy deposits is largely limited to near surface features (<15 feet depth). This is key since the battlefield contained cottonwood trees that only grow on sandy areas. Limited coring combined with ERI methods can delineate the potential areas for the entire 1868 channel provided that the sandy deposits from that channel are still located in the battlefield area.

Secondly, the Washita River appears to be dependent on ground water on the site to maintain flow. Only during extreme high flow events does the system recharge the deeper ground water system, and only in some areas. Even during high flow events, much of the ground water system continues discharging into the river. The river discharge appears to be dominantly a function of the level of the ground water system.

What does this relationship between the ground water and surface water indicate for conditions in 1868? If land use in the area has not caused significant changes to the ground water system, it is expected that the Washita River was a discharge zone for ground water in 1868. The waters that were present at Black Kettle's campsite could have reasonably been assumed to be comprised of discharging ground water that was slightly colder than the mean annual temperature of the area. The cottonwoods would have been limited to narrow bands on the site where sufficient sand deposits allowed them to grow. The geologic structure and hydrogeologic setting for the WBNHS likely provided the framework for the streamflow and cottonwood ecology for the battlefield.

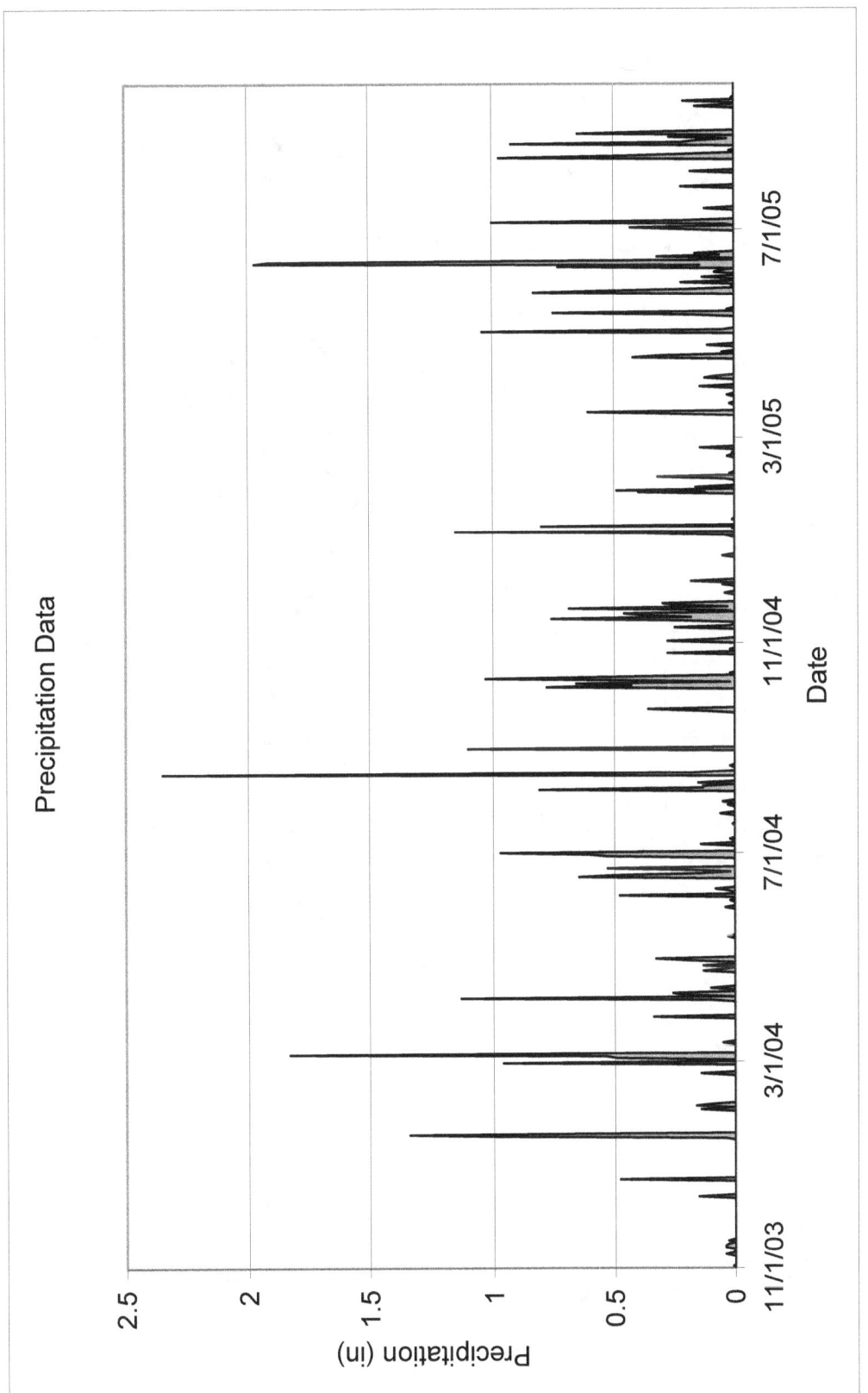

Figure 12. Precipitation record for Cheyenne, OK, during study period (Mesonet).

21

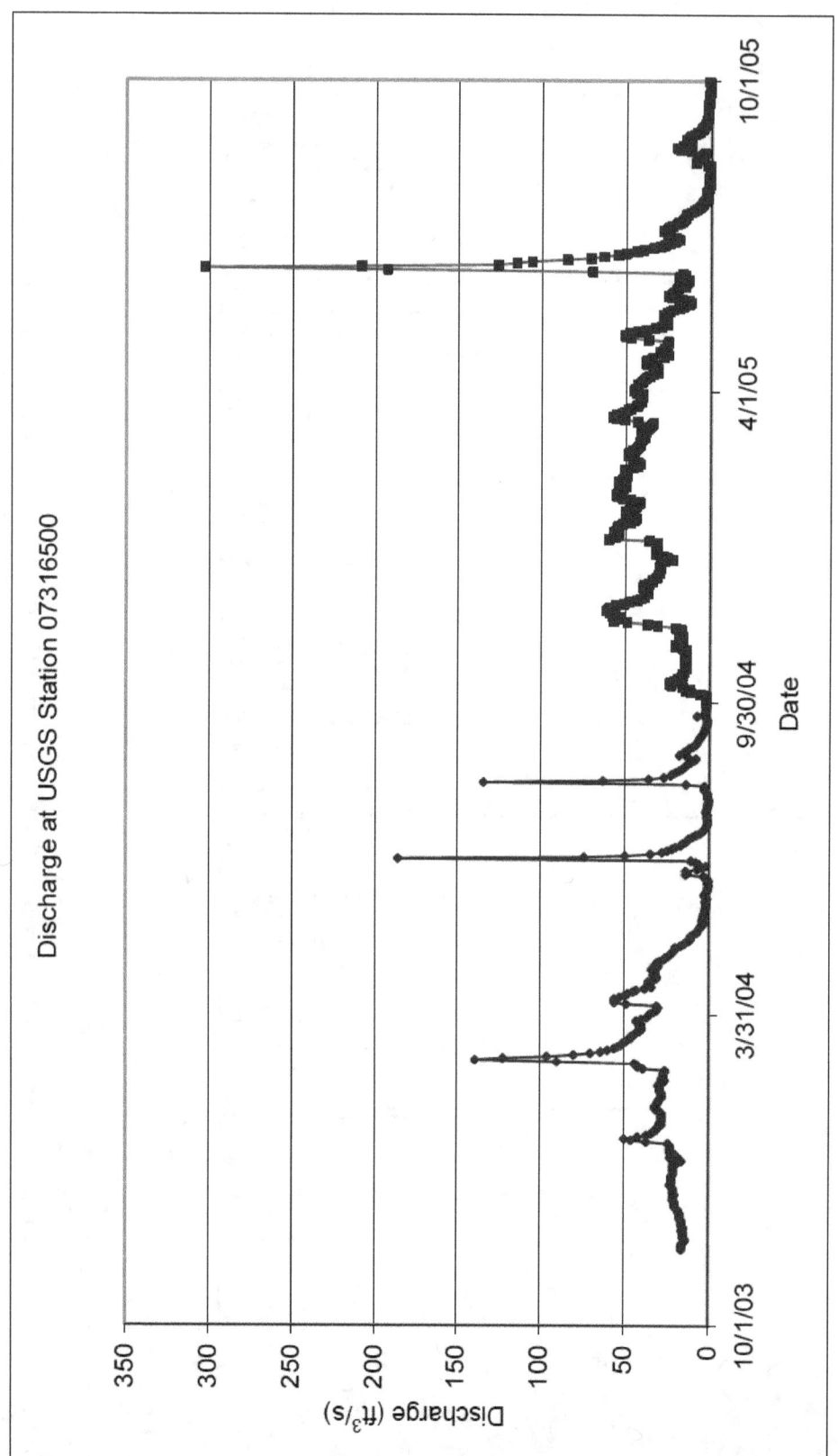

Figure 13. Stream discharge at U.S. Geological Survey gauging station at Cheyenne, OK, during study period.

22

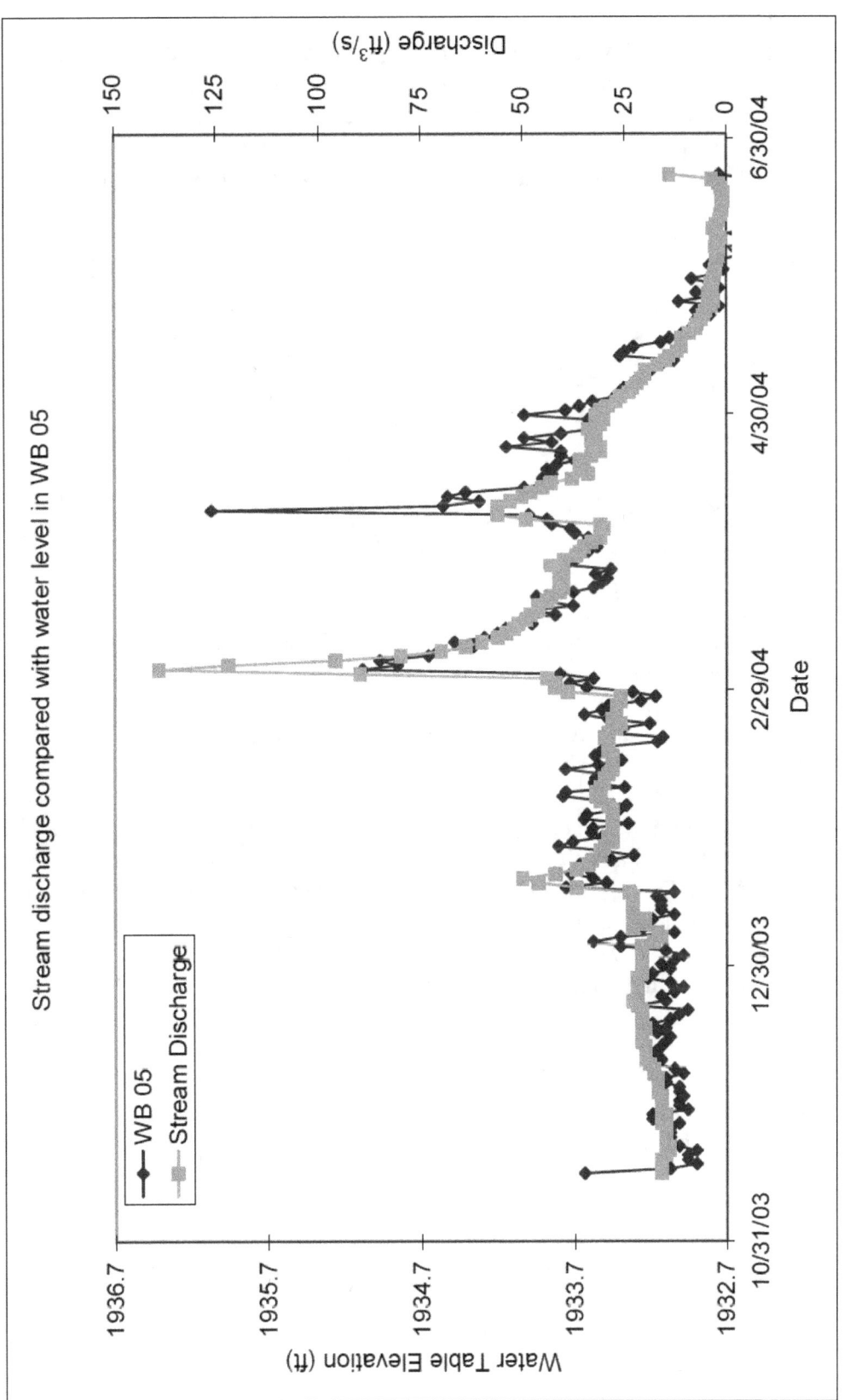

Figure 14. Comparison of Washita River stream discharge and water level in Well WB 05.

23

5.2 Results for Objective #2: Channel Adjustment over Time

Historical documents, summarized by Greene (2004), helped to document changes in channel morphology of the Washita River since the 1868 battle. New interpretations have been added based on our analyses of aerial photos, gaging station records, the Wisleder (2004) thesis, and electrical resistivity data. At the time of the battle, Black Kettle's village covered 25 acres on the south side of the river (Figure 15). The channel was 3-4 meters wide, with steep banks exposed at low flow.

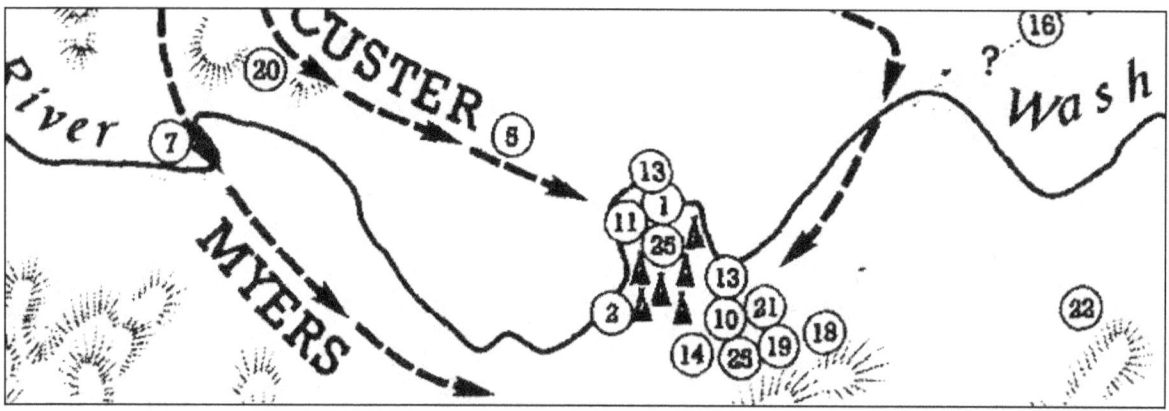

Figure 15. Sketch map of the Washita River and the 1868 battle, showing the location of Black Kettle's village (Barde, ca. 1900).

By 1904-1910, most of the trees had been felled along the river. The battle site on the floodplain had not yet been plowed. The gooseneck meander bend still existed that had flanked Black Kettle's campsite (Figure 15). Between 1910-1930, two artificial meander cutoffs were created for the convenience of irrigation farmers (Figure 16). The former meander loop is revealed by electrical resistivity line WB-1-05 and WB-3-05, evident in Figure 5 and two electrical resistivity profiles (Figures C3 and C5). During the 1930s, the Washita River was affected by floods and delivery of massive amounts of sediment. The Washita River became a wide-shallow, braided channel. Bankfull width was up to 0.4 km (Figure 17). It was most likely a Rosgen type D5 or F5 during the Dust Bowl period. Large areas in the active channel were unvegetated (Figures 16-18).

Beginning in the 1930s, 63 flood control structures were built upstream of the WBNHS by the Natural Resources Conservation Service and U.S. Army Corps of Engineers. These structures were designed to control peak flows, trap sediment, and improve channel stability. Simultaneously, hundreds of cattle ponds were installed, which also detained storm period runoff and sediment. The net effect of these structures in decreasing peak flows is illustrated by the data in Table 3.

Wisleder (2004), as part of this study, evaluated the effects of reservoirs in trapping sediment along the upper Washita River watershed. Wisleder conducted field measurements of sedimentation behind the dams and applied the WEPP model, developed at Purdue University, to determine if watershed condition affected sedimentation. The WEPP model was found to severely underestimate sediment in each reservoir, because the model does not measure sediment from unpaved roads, which is a significant source of sediment in this region. Wisleder found

Figure 16. 1961 aerial photograph of the WBHNS acquired 30 June 1961 (streamflow = 19 cfs) (ASCS). The artificial cut-off of the gooseneck meander is in the right-most one-third of the figure. Remnants of the former meander loop are reflected in the arcuate vegetation pattern. White areas are unvegetated sand bars. The site of Black Kettle's village is shown in the oval; by 1961, and in times since, the village site is north of the river.

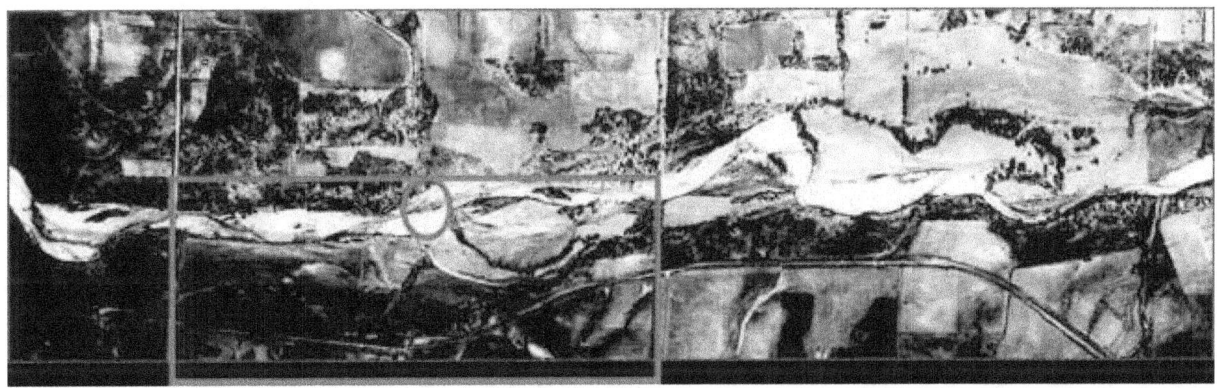

Figure 17. 1936 aerial photo acquired 31 December 1936 (National Archives). White areas are unvegetated sand bars. The site of Black Kettle's village is shown in the oval; in 1936, this was in the active channel.

Table 4. Reduction in peak flows after period of dam building in upper Washita River watershed (Tortonelli, 2002).

Period	2-yr Flood (cfs)	5-yr Flood (cfs)	10-yr Flood (cfs)	25-yr Flood (cfs)	50-yr Flood (cfs)	100-yr Flood (cfs)
1934-1960	5,500	15,400	26,900	49,200	73,200	105,000
1961-1999	696	2,010	3,540	6,570	9,850	14,200

77.5% of the residual variation could be explained by considering length of section line roads in each watershed. In addition, all flood control dams measured were found to be filled to only a fraction of their sediment storage capacity, or to contain immeasurably small amounts. It could be concluded that changes in land use–from wheat fields to pastureland–had more to do with the decreased sediment load to the Washita River than did the dams.

By 1961 the Washita River had returned to its pre-Dust Bowl morphology as a single-thread, sinuous channel (Figure 16). Vegetation had encroached on the active channel.

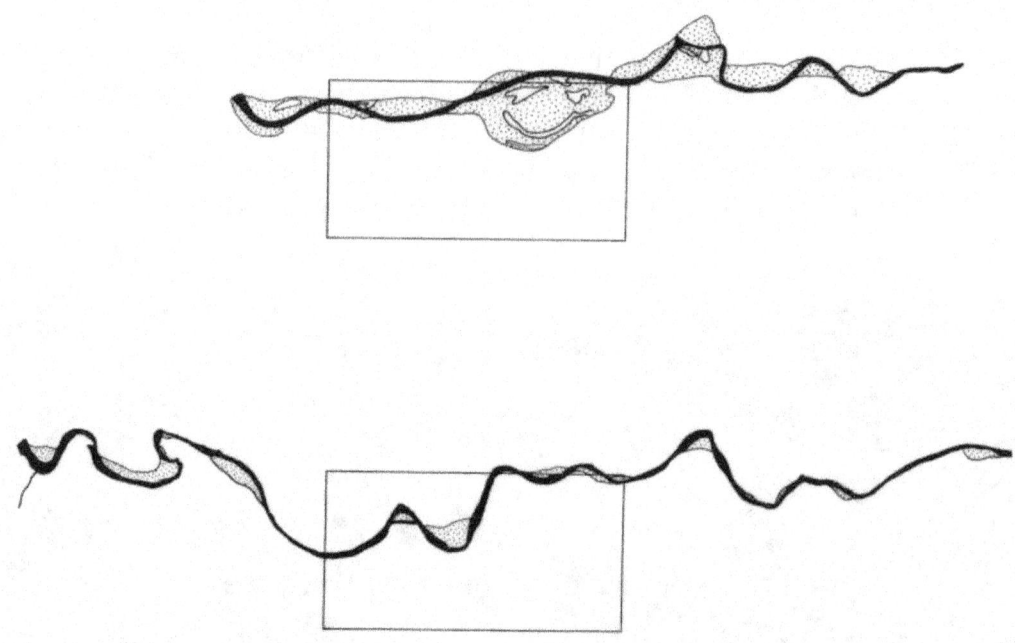

Figure 18. Comparison of the 1936 channel (above) and the 1961 channel (bottom). The boundaries of the WBNHS are shown as a box (0.5 mi. x 1 mi.) for reference. The stippled areas indicate unvegetated sand bars.

In the period 1961-1999, only very minor changes were observed in plan view channel pattern of the Washita River. The channel continued to become more narrow as vegetation encroached on the channel in the absence of high peak flows. At the present time, the Washita River in the WBNHS is a single-thread, sand channel with moderate entrenchment, moderate width-to-depth ratio, and sinuosity characteristic of a Rosgen type B5 channel. Reach # 1 is cut in more clay-rich sediments, as reflected in the electrical resistivity data (Figure C1), and the channel banks are steeper, as one would expect. Reach # 4 is carved in more sand-rich sediments, again reflected in the electrical resistivity data (Figure C2), so the channel is wider and banks are not as steep.

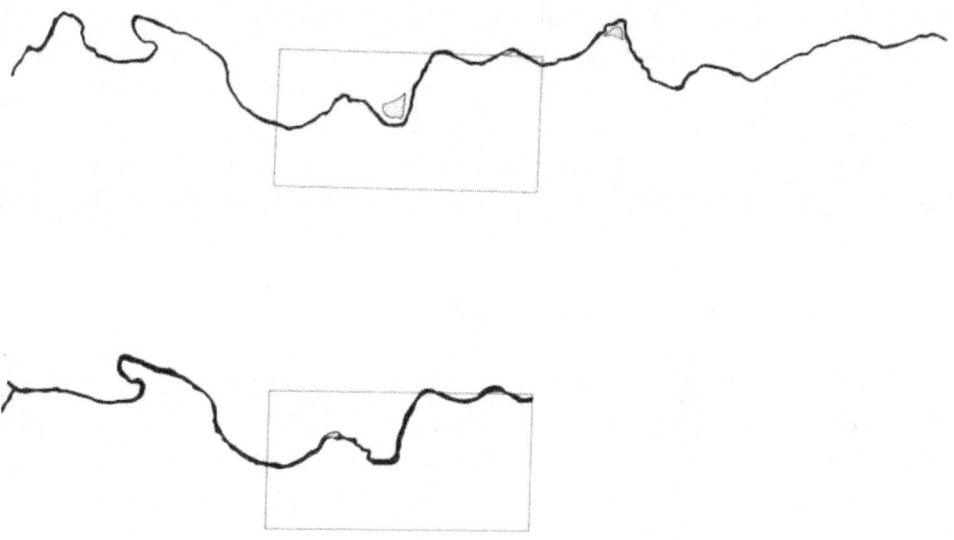

Figure 19. Comparison of the 1982 channel (above, Q = 13 cfs) and the 1999 channel (bottom, Q = 47 cfs). The boundaries of the WBNHS are shown as a box (0.5 mi. x 1 mi.) for reference.

5.3   Results for Objective #3: 1868 Channel vs. Present-Day Conditions

The present-day Washita River in the WBNHS is surprisingly close to the channel that existed in 1868. Both in 1868 and at the present, the Washita River is a single-thread, sinuous, sand-bed channel, with a width-to-depth ratio and degree of entrenchment that is described as a Rosgen B5 type channel. The channel is somewhat more entrenched in the western end of the WBNHS (Reach #1) than the other reaches because of the higher silt-clay in the floodplain sediments, which creates steep, high stream banks. On the eastern end of the WBNHS (Reach #4), the channel is cut into sandier material and has a form that is generally wider and more shallow (Figures C1 and C2). The hydrologic regime of peak flows and sediment load is entirely different today than what existed in 1868 because of the changes in the watershed involving dams and land use. Groundwater is discharging into the Washita River as it probably did in the past, hence the close correlation between streamflow and water table elevation. Because the channel in Reach #1 is slightly more entrenched, the alluvial water table is closer to the stream in Reach #4 than in Reach #1. Therefore, it is entirely understandable why cottonwoods are thriving in Reach #4 and less so in Reach #1. Cottonwoods need seed beds (i.e., point bars or low terraces) that are approximately one meter above the active channel–bare, moist sites that are protected from intense physical disturbance. However, if water table drops greater than 2.5 meters below the tap roots of cottonwoods, survival is doubtful (Scott et al. 1997, Cooper et al. 1999).

5.4   Results for Objective #4: Alternatives for a Stable Modern-Day Channel

Re-establishing cottonwood trees is seen as a key to achieving a properly functioning channel-riparian system along the Washita River in the WNHHS. This is more likely to occur in Reach #4 than in the other reaches. In Reach #1, the channel is entrenched and there are no point bars to form seed-beds. In Reaches #1-3, tamarisk is competing with cottonwoods for riparian space, and beavers (or other browsers) are damaging cottonwood trees when they do get established. Cottonwood trees should be reintroduced along the banks and in the floodplain of the Washita River in the WBNHS. However, plantings must be accompanied by tamarisk control and measures to protect cottonwoods from browsers. In addition, large woody debris should be artificially introduced to the channel to create more flow deflection against banks, with point bars as a result. Some of these point bars could provide the necessary seed beds for cottonwoods in all four reaches. Plantings will be necessary in the short term because of the lack of mature trees as a seed source.

The location of Black Kettle's village is now on the north side of the river, contrary to 1868, because of meander migration and artificial cutoffs. One possible action to create an 1868 channel would be to re-open the abandoned meander loop (Figures 16 and 18). However, this would constitute a fairly drastic measure when one cannot also re-create the flow and sediment regime of 1868. Instead, the WBNHS should create an educational display that describes and explains the channel changes since 1868 and what they mean for locating Black Kettle's village.

6. Conclusions

The WBNHS retains some of its original integrity, but changes in agricultural practices (wheat fields to pastureland) and flood control projects in the 1950s on tributaries have altered the channel and riparian vegetation. Some channel change may also be attributed to Dust Bowl period disturbances in the 1930s as poor agricultural practices led to excessive sediment supply and frequent flash floods (Cooke and Reeves 1976). Other channel changes are the result of direct channel diversions, straightening, or narrowing by farmers. In the 1940s, the channel assumed a braided pattern with ephemeral or seasonal flow (Rosgen D5 or F5 channel type). Soil conservation efforts in the subsequent decades have reduced sediment supply and reduced the magnitudes and frequency of floods. Even with all of the drastic changes in watershed controls, the present day channel is surprisingly similar in plan view form and channel cross-sectional characteristics to what existed in 1868. The main differences are as follows: 1) slightly greater entrenchment in Reach #1 (with related lack of point bars); 2) absence of mature cottonwoods in Reaches 1-3 (because of browsing and competition from tamarisk); 3) absence of large woody debris to help create point bars as seed beds for cottonwoods; and 4) lateral stream mobility has been altered by artificial cutoffs and recent decline in peak flows.

At least three future actions or alternatives could be considered for the Washita River: 1) no action (let nature take its course); 2) plant cottonwoods and import large woody debris at critical locations to support a stable channel form; and 3) relocate the channel to better reflect the 1868 channel form and location with respect to Black Kettle's camp. If no action is taken (alternative #1), cottonwoods will continue to disappear because of browsing by beaver, invasion of tamarisk, and lack of a suitable seedbed (unvegetated sand bars) for new growth.

Planting of cottonwoods (alternative #2) is recommended in Reaches #2 and #3 if also accompanied by control of browsers and tamarisk invasion. Cottonwoods are fairly well established in Reach # 4, so new plantings are probably not needed. Plantings could be pursued in Reach # 1 if the channel bed is raised by installing log steps, or the higher south banks are bulldozed to a lower elevation, but the channel morphology is still not likely to support cottonwood propagation over the long haul in Reach # 1. Log steps will be difficult to stabilize, and vegetation encroachment on sand bars will be difficult to reverse. Instead, large woody debris should be placed in Reaches #2 and #3 to enhance formation of point bars. Cottonwoods should be planted on low (less than one meter high) cut banks and above the bankfull stage on sandy point bars. In all cases, cottonwoods should be planted so roots can extend to the water table. Groundwater is discharging into the Washita River, so the alluvial water table is well within the reach of roots.

Alternative #3 is technically possible, now that the location of the 1868 channel has been identified. On the one hand, it might be considered aesthetically pleasing and historically accurate for visitors to view the site of Black Kettle's camp where it existed in 1868 relative to the river. On the other hand, relocating the river to its 1868 position would involve major disturbance of the present floodplain by earth-moving equipment and require a sophisticated degree of river engineering to produce a stable channel that resembles the 1868 in cross-section shape. Moreover, the new channel dimensions (gradient, cross-sectional shape, sinuosity) would not have adjusted to the regime of water and sediment that has prevailed since the era of upstream dam building and upland conversion from cropland to pasture. Instead, the story of the metamorphosis of the Washita River could be used for educational purposes as part of the park interpretative activities.

7. References

Barde, Fred S. Circa 1900. *Map in* Fred S. Barde Collection. Archives and Manuscript Division, Oklahoma Historical Society, Oklahoma City. 82.80, Box 42, No. 3 (oversized).

Cooke, R. U., and R. W. Reeves. 1976. Arroyos and environmental change in the American Southwest. Oxford University Press, London, England.

Cooper, D. J., D. M. Merritt, D. C. Andersen, and R. A. Chimner. 1999. Factors controlling the reestablishment of Fremont cottonwood seedlings on the upper Green River, USA. Regulated Rivers-Research and Management 15:419-440.

Graf, W. L. 1984. A probabilistic approach to the spatial assessment of river channel instability. Water Resources Research 20:953-962.

Greene, J. A. 2004. Washita—The U.S. Army and the Southern Cheyennes, 1867-1869. University of Oklahoma Press, Norman.

Hoagland, B. W., A. Buthod, and W. Elisens. 2005. Vascular flora and historic vegetation of the Washita Battlefield National Historic Site, Roger Mills County, Oklahoma. Unpublished final project report submitted to the National Park Service.

Inglis, R. and J. Wagner. 2001. Trip report for travel to the Washita Battlefield July 16-19, 2001: Memorandum to superintendent, Washita Battlefield National Historic Site. National Park Service, Natural Resources Program Center, Water Resources Division, Fort Collins, CO.

Lees, W. B., D. D. Scott, B. Rea, and C. V. Haynes. 1997. Archaeology of the Washita Battlefield National Historical Site. Oklahoma Historical Society, Oklahoma City, OK.

Platts, W. S., C. Armour, G. D. Booth, M. Bryant, J. Bufford, P. Cuplin, S. Jensen, G. W. Lienkaemper, G. W. Minshall, S. B. Monsen, R. L. Nelson, J. R. Sedell, and J. S. Tuhy. 1987. Methods for evaluating riparian habitats with applications to management. USFS, Intermountain Research Station. General Technical Report INT-221.

Reber, J., M. Flora, and J. Harte. 1999. Washita Battlefield National Historic Site, Oklahoma. Water Resources Scoping Report NPS/NRWRS/NRTR-99/235. National Park Service, Natural Resource Program Center, Water Resources Division, Fort Collins, CO

Richards, K. 1982. Rivers: Form and process in alluvial channels. Methuen, London, England.

Schumm, S. A. 1991. To interpret the earth: Ten ways to be wrong. Cambridge University Press, Cambridge, England.

Tortonelli, R. L. 2002. Statistical summaries of streamflow in Oklahoma through 1999. US Geological Survey. Water Resources Investigations Report 02-4025:390-393.

Wisleder, D. R. 2004. Reservoir sedimentation along the upper Washita River in western Oklahoma and northern Texas. M.S. Thesis in Geography, Oklahoma State University: Stillwater, OK.

APPENDIX A: CROSS-SECTIONS

Appendix A1. Cross-section profiles for three cross-sections upstream of WBNHS. Refer to Figure 3 and Table 2 for locations and substrate characteristics, respectively. No permanent markers were established, but the GPS coordinates of each cross-section are given.

Moving from East to West

WoB T1

	Looking upstream, left	
GPS	Latitude	Longitude
	35°	99°
	37.248	42.847

Point	Distance	Elevation
1	0	589.7198
2	2.3	588.9598
3	4.4	588.9298
4	6.4	588.9098
5	8.4	588.9498
6	12.3	589.6098

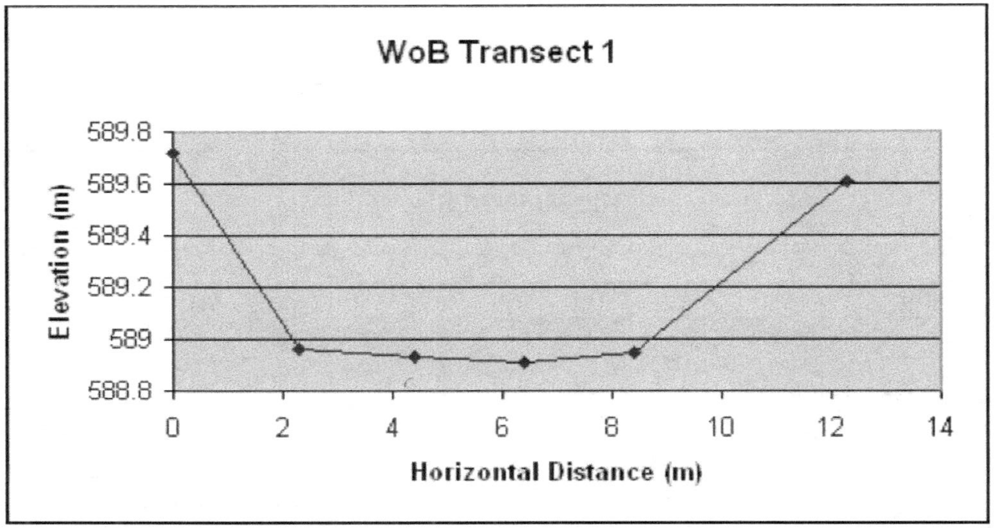

WoB Transect 1

35

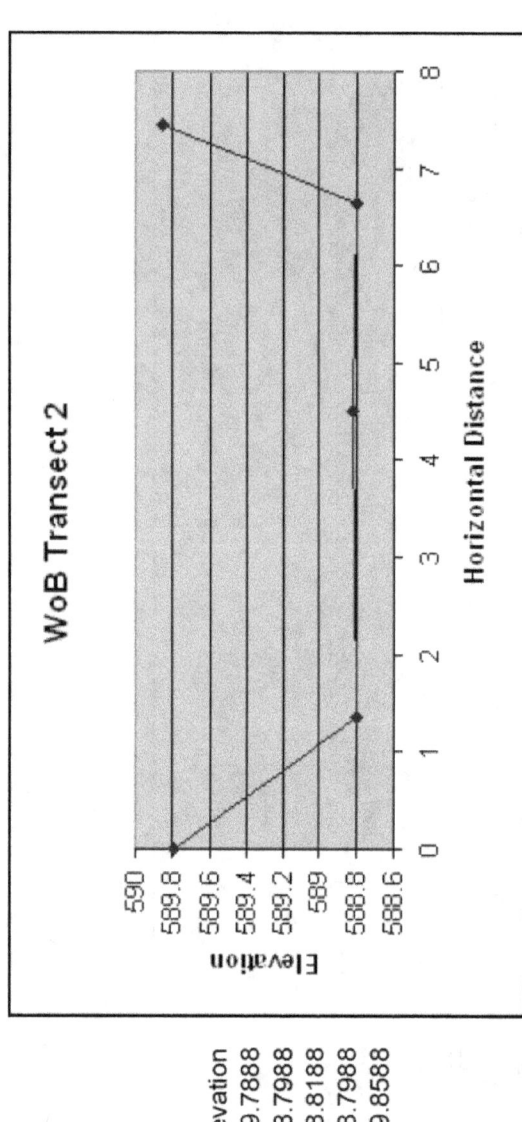

WoB Transect 2

Point	Distance	Elevation
1	0	589.7888
2	1.35	588.7988
3	4.5	588.8188
4	6.65	588.7988
5	7.45	589.8588

WoB T2   Looking upstream, left

GPS	Latitude	Longitude
	n/a	n/a

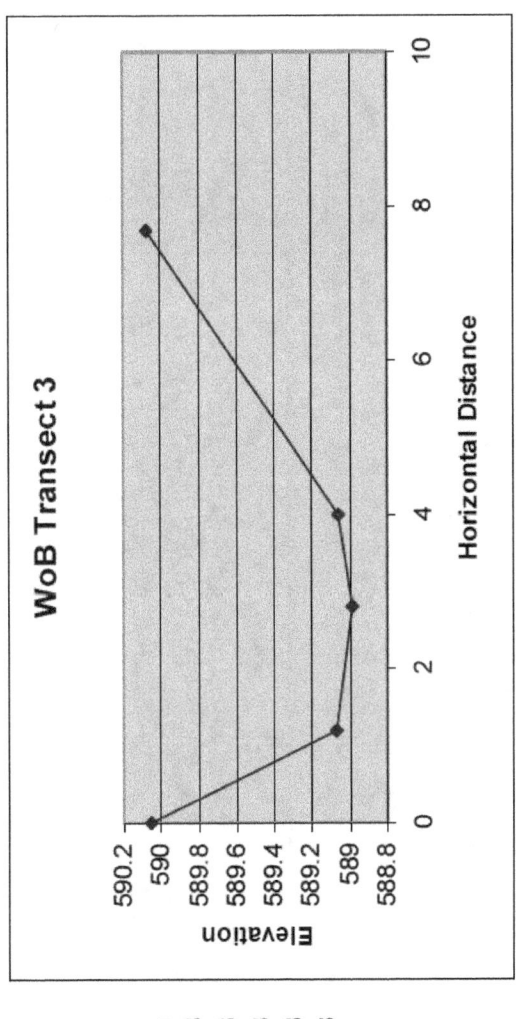

WoB T3   Looking upstream, left

GPS	Latitude	Longitude
	n/a	n/a

Point	Distance	Elevation
1	0	590.0588
2	1.2	589.0688
3	2.8	588.9888
4	4	589.0588
5	7.7	590.0788

Appendix A2. Cross-section profiles for six cross-sections in Reach #1 of WBNHS. Refer to Figure 3 and Table 2 for locations and substrate characteristics, respectively.

Moving from East to West

Transect 1	Looking upstream, left		
GPS	Latitude	Longitude	
	35° 37.222	99° 42.762	
Point	Distance	Difference	Elevation
1	0	1.37	590.6088
2	1.6	3.24	588.7388
3	3	3.19	588.7888
4	4.75	3.3	588.6788
5	6.1	3.27	588.7088
6	8.1	3.2	588.7788
7	9.2	2	589.9788

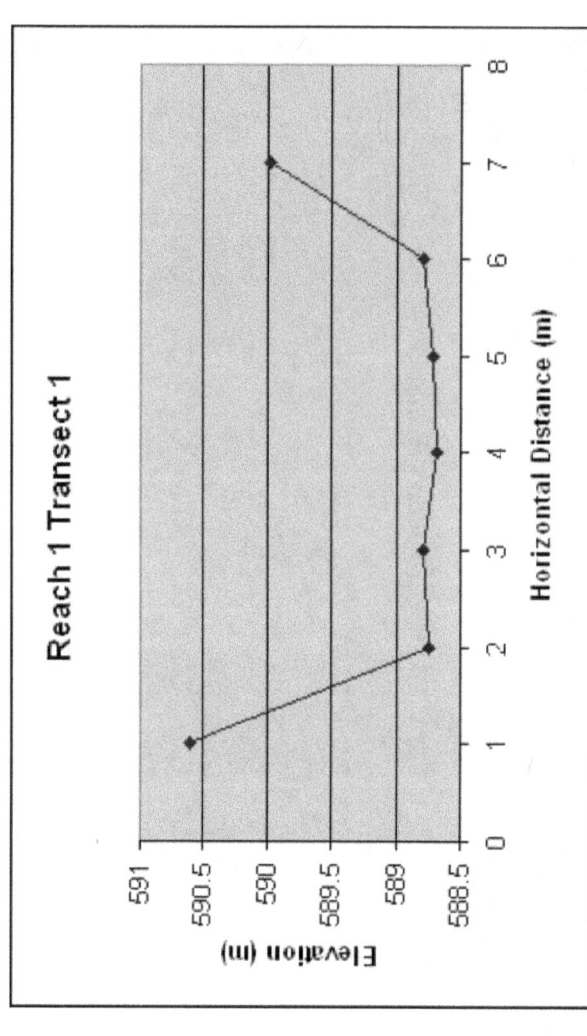

Reach 1 Transect 1

Transect 2   Looking upstream, left

GPS   Latitude   Longitude
       35° 37.236 99° 42.793

Point	Distance	Difference	Elevation
1	0	2.01	589.9688
2	1.7	3.28	588.6988
3	2.4	3.25	588.7288
4	4.5	3.14	588.8388
5	6.4	3.2	588.7788
6	8	2.2	589.7788

Reach 1 Transect 2

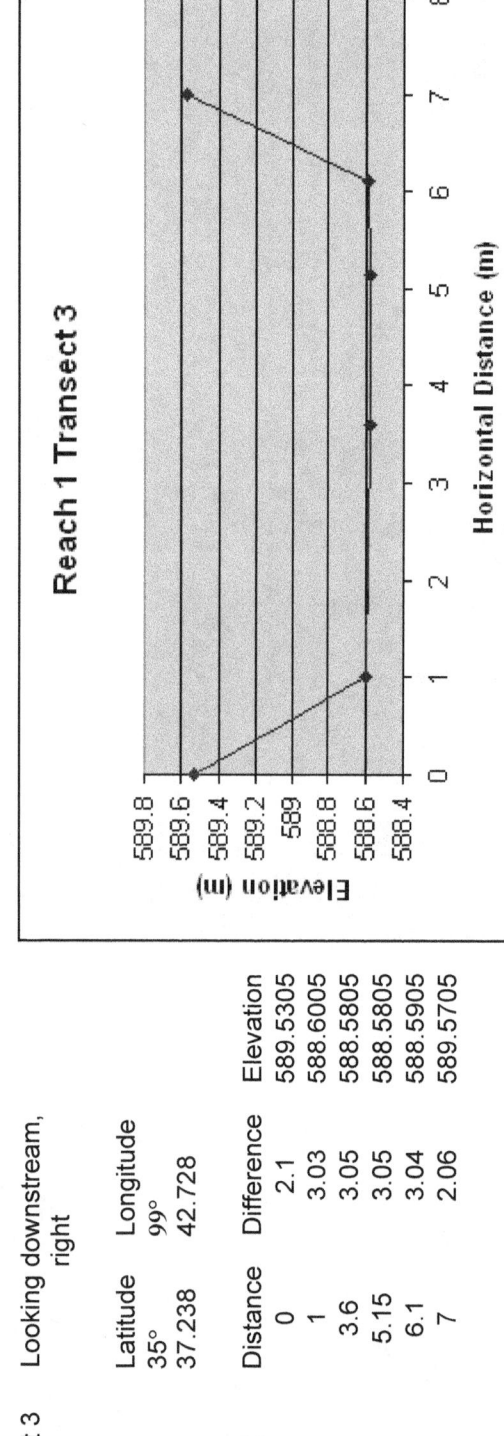

Reach 1 Transect 3

Transect 3   Looking downstream, right

GPS   Latitude   Longitude
       35°   99°
       37.238   42.728

Point	Distance	Difference	Elevation
1	0	2.1	589.5305
2	1	3.03	588.6005
3	3.6	3.05	588.5805
4	5.15	3.05	588.5805
5	6.1	3.04	588.5905
6	7	2.06	589.5705

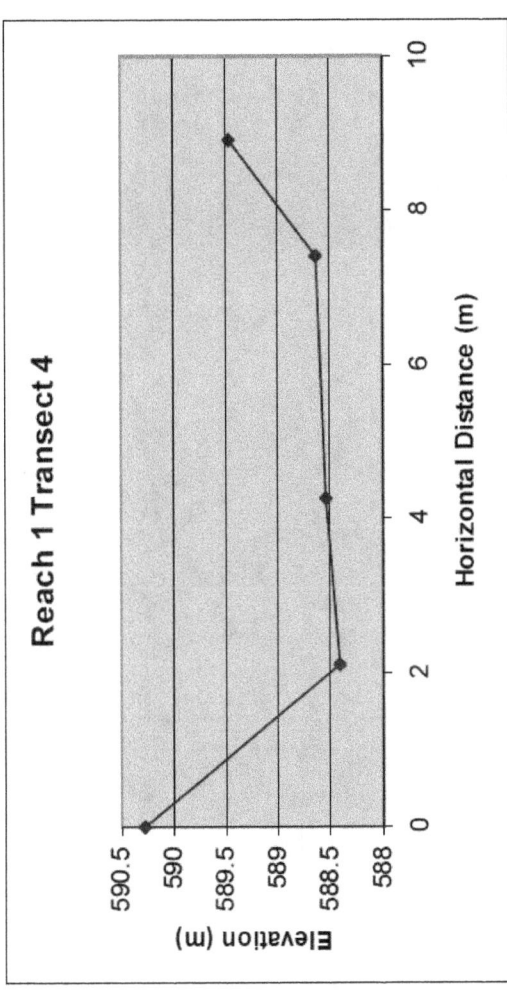

Reach 1 Transect 4

Transect 4   Looking downstream, right

GPS	Latitude 35° 37.241	Longitude 99° 42.692		
Point		Distance	Difference	Elevation
1		0	1.35	590.2805
2		2.1	3.22	588.4105
3		4.25	3.1	588.5305
4		7.4	3.01	588.6205
5		8.9	2.16	589.4705

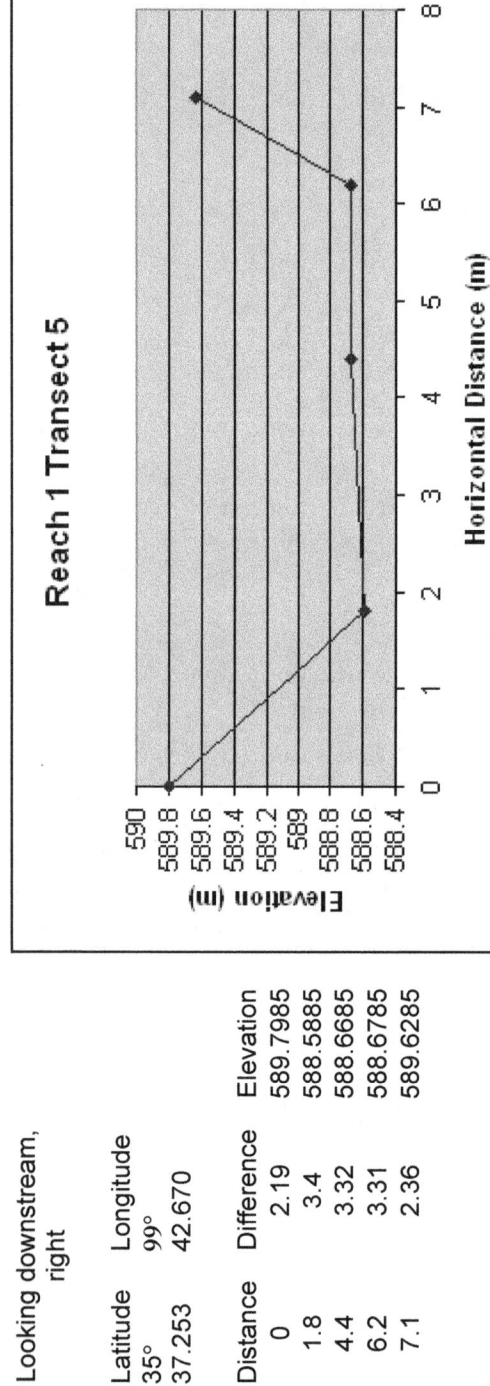

Reach 1 Transect 5

Transect 5	Looking downstream, right		
GPS		Latitude 35° 37.253	Longitude 99° 42.670

Point	Distance	Difference	Elevation
1	0	2.19	589.7985
2	1.8	3.4	588.5885
3	4.4	3.32	588.6685
4	6.2	3.31	588.6785
5	7.1	2.36	589.6285

42

Transect 6   Looking downstream, right

GPS   Latitude   Longitude
       35° 37.267   99° 42.638

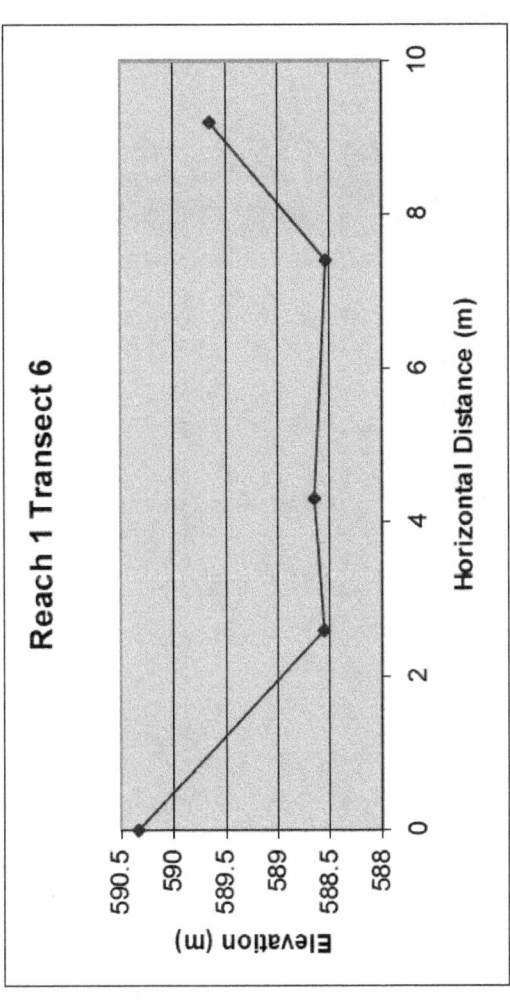

Point	Distance	Difference	Elevation
1	0	0.87	590.3388
2	2.6	2.66	588.5488
3	4.3	2.56	588.6488
4	7.4	2.67	588.5388
5	9.2	1.56	589.6488

Appendix A3. Cross-section profiles for six cross-sections in Reach #2 of WBNHS. Refer to Figure 3 and Table 2 for locations and substrate characteristics, respectively.

Transect 1   Looking downstream, right

GPS   Latitude   Longitude
             35° 37.284   99° 42.608

Point	Distance	Difference	Elevation
1	0	1.32	589.8888
2	1.8	2.87	588.3388
3	4.8	2.69	588.5188
4	6.7	2.39	588.8188
5	8.1	1.95	589.2588

Reach 2 Transect 1

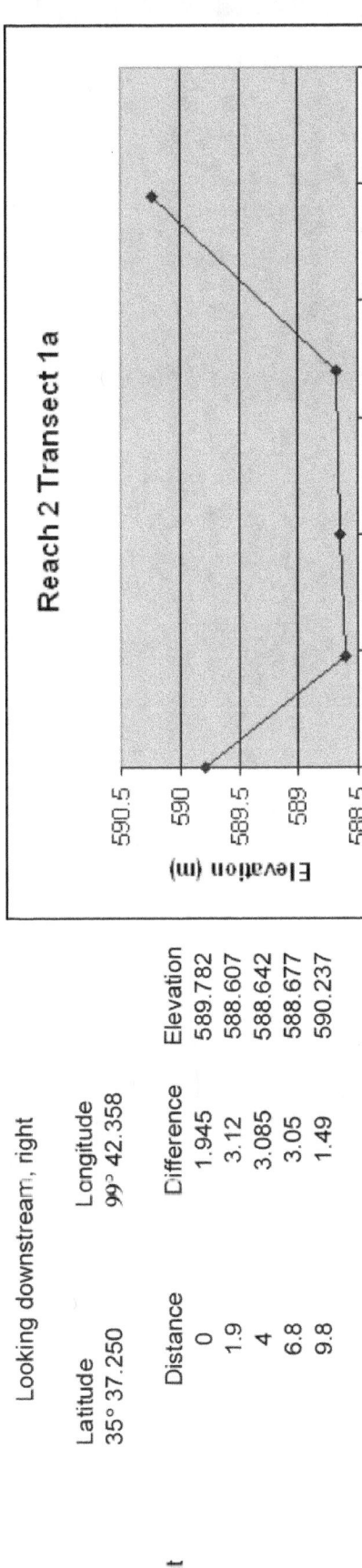

Reach 2 Transect 1a

Transect 1a

GPS

Looking downstream, right

	Latitude	Longitude	
	35° 37.250	99° 42.358	
Point	Distance	Difference	Elevation
1	0	1.945	589.782
2	1.9	3.12	588.607
3	4	3.085	588.642
4	6.8	3.05	588.677
5	9.8	1.49	590.237

45

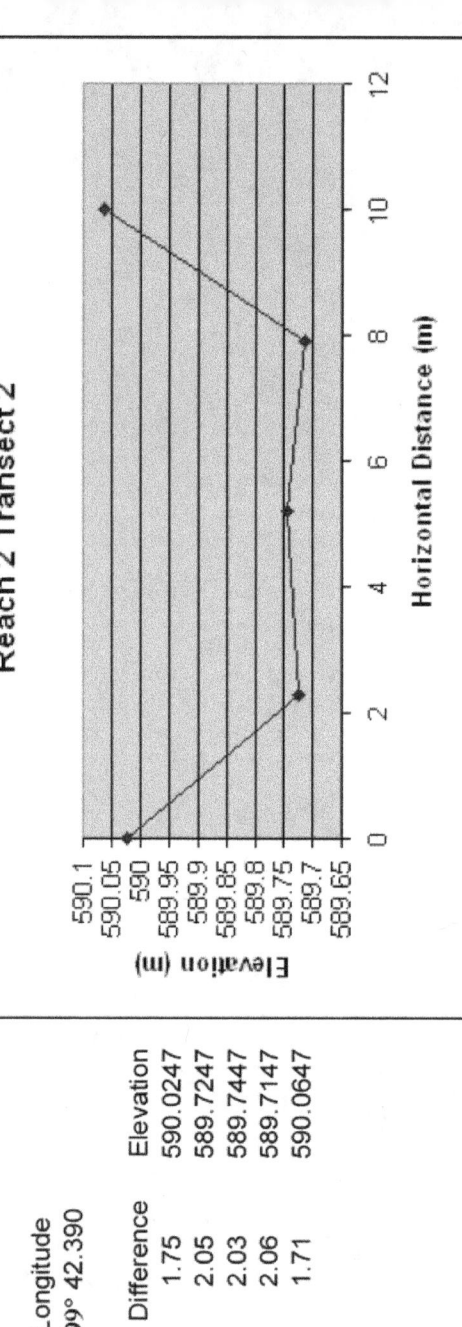

Reach 2 Transect 2

Transect 2

GPS

Looking downstream, right

	Latitude	Longitude	
	35° 37.270	99° 42.390	

Point	Distance	Difference	Elevation
1	0	1.75	590.0247
2	2.3	2.05	589.7247
3	5.2	2.03	589.7447
4	7.9	2.06	589.7147
5	10	1.71	590.0647

Transect 3

Looking downstream, right

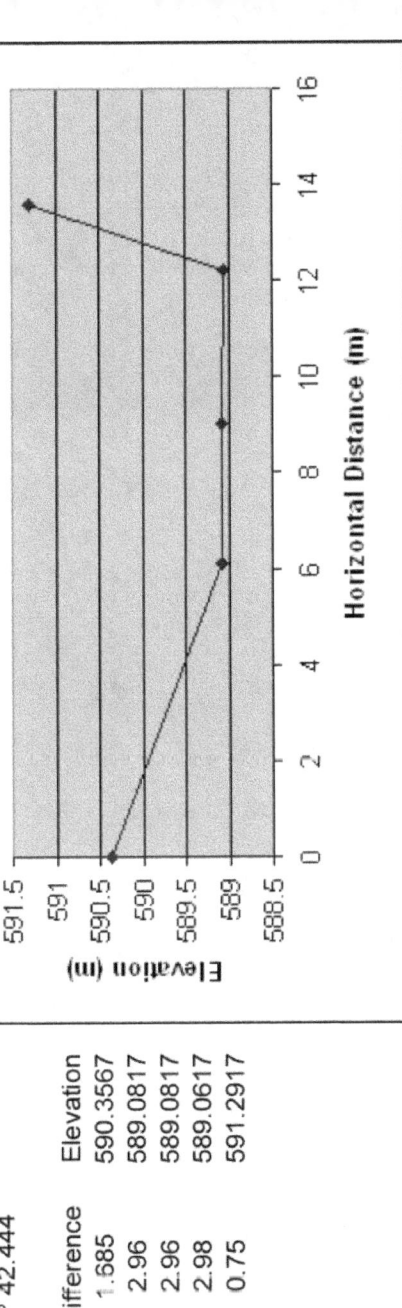

GPS	Latitude	Longitude
	35° 37.319	99° 42.444

Point	Distance	Difference	Elevation
1	0	1.685	590.3567
2	6.1	2.96	589.0817
3	9	2.96	589.0817
4	12.2	2.98	589.0617
5	13.6	0.75	591.2917

Transect 4

Looking downstream, right

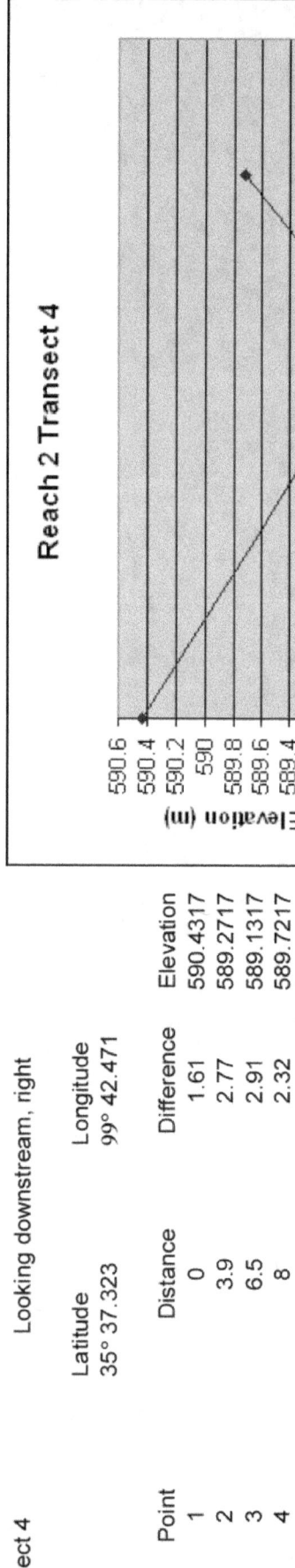

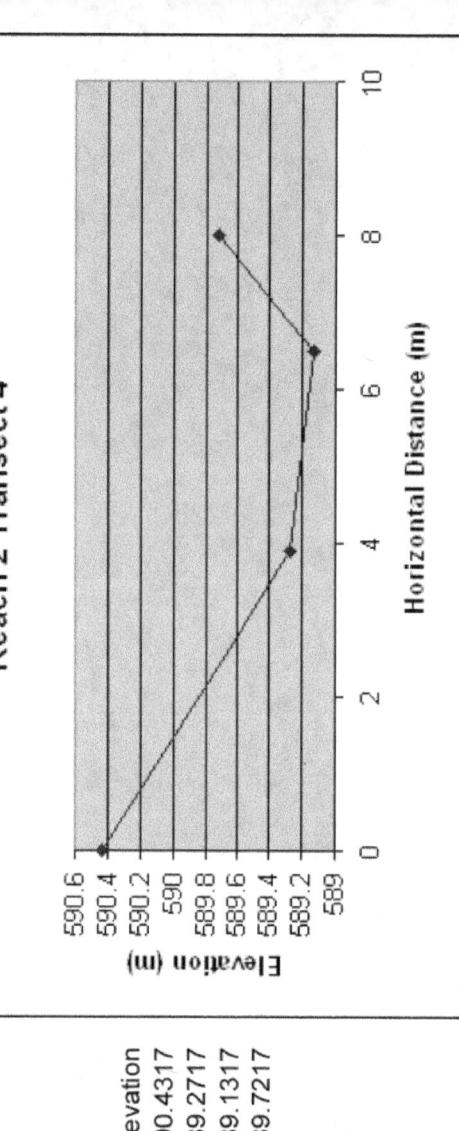

GPS

	Latitude 35° 37.323	Longitude 99° 42.471		
Point	Distance	Difference	Elevation	
1	0	1.61	590.4317	
2	3.9	2.77	589.2717	
3	6.5	2.91	589.1317	
4	8	2.32	589.7217	

Appendix A4. Cross-section profiles for six cross-sections in Reach #3 of WBNHS. Refer to Figure 3 and Table 2 for locations and substrate characteristics, respectively.

Moving from East to West

Reach 3 Transect 1

Transect 1		Looking downstream, right	
GPS	Latitude	Longitude	
	35° 37.434	99° 41.210	
Point	Distance	Difference	Elevation
1	0	2.21	588.7247
2	1.4	3.32	587.6147
3	4.3	3.32	587.6147
4	7.3	3.325	587.6097
5	8.5	2.035	588.8997

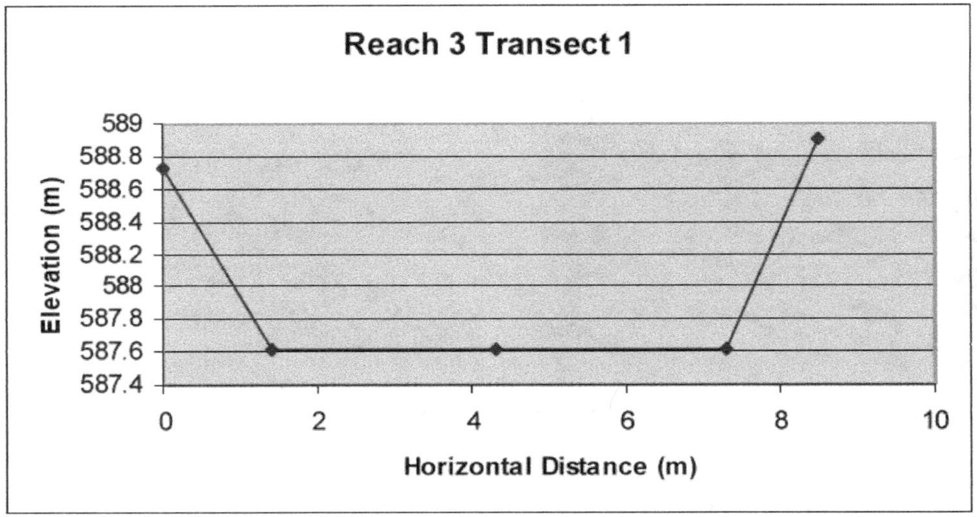

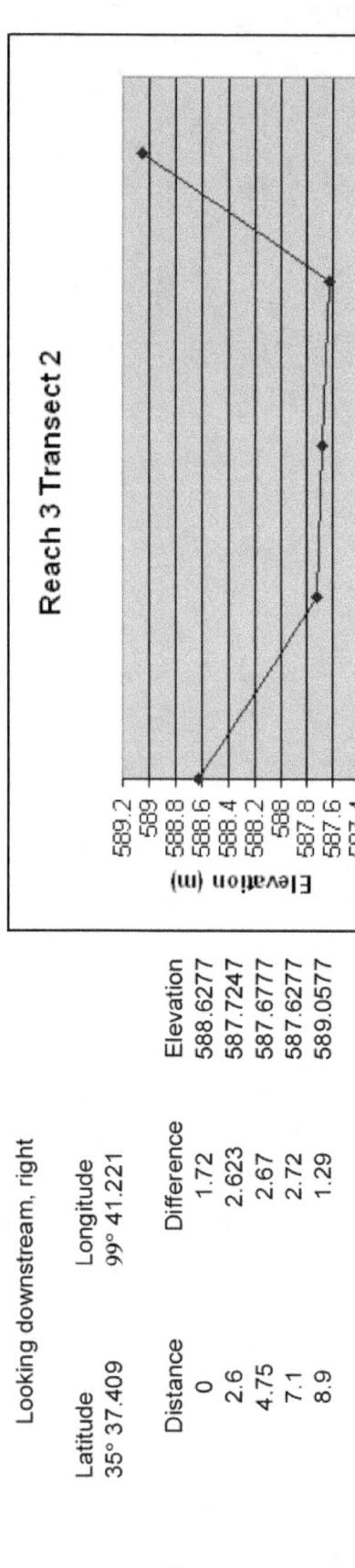

Reach 3 Transect 2

Transect 2		Looking downstream, right		
GPS		Latitude	Longitude	
		35° 37.409	99° 41.221	
	Point	Distance	Difference	Elevation
	1	0	1.72	588.6277
	2	2.6	2.623	587.7247
	3	4.75	2.67	587.6777
	4	7.1	2.72	587.6277
	5	8.9	1.29	589.0577

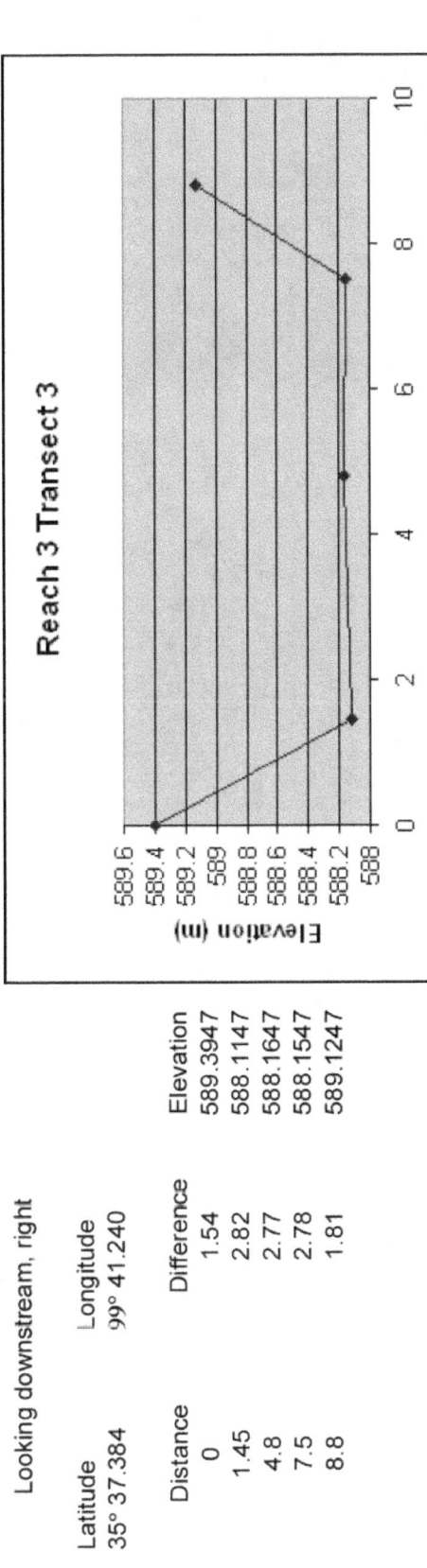

Reach 3 Transect 3

Transect 3		Looking downstream, right		
GPS		Latitude	Longitude	
		35° 37.384	99° 41.240	
	Point	Distance	Difference	Elevation
	1	0	1.54	589.3947
	2	1.45	2.82	588.1147
	3	4.8	2.77	588.1647
	4	7.5	2.78	588.1547
	5	8.8	1.81	589.1247

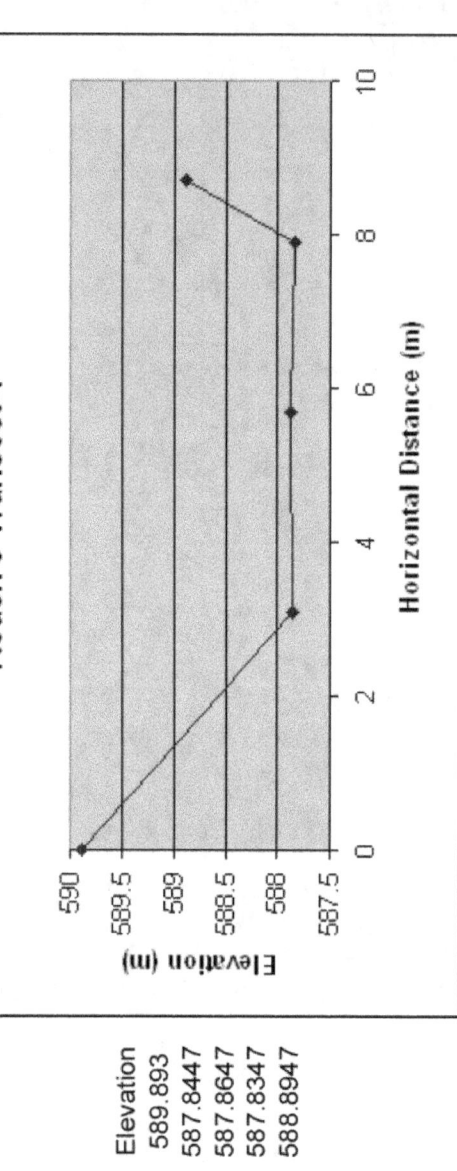

Reach 3 Transect 4

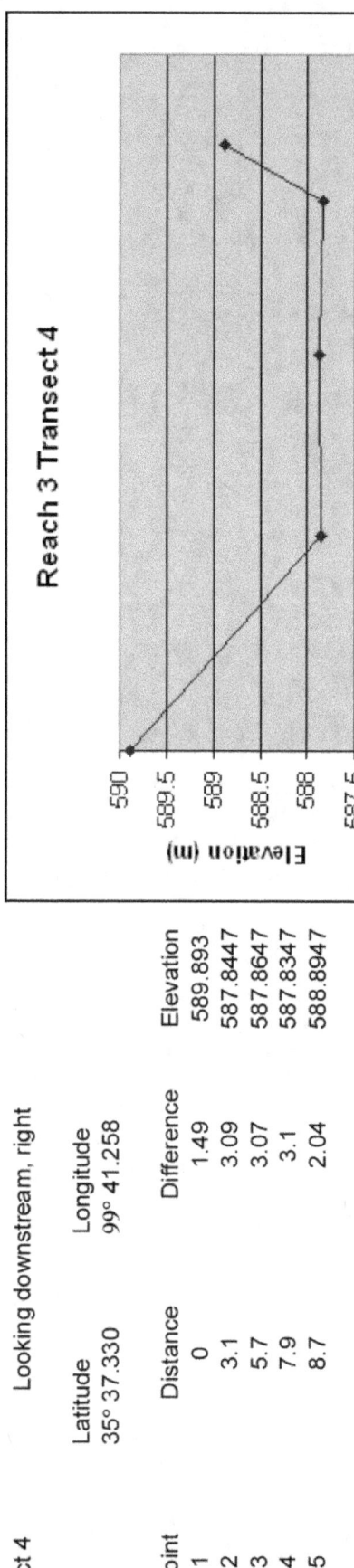

Transect 4	Looking downstream, right			
GPS	Latitude 35° 37.330	Longitude 99° 41.258		
Point		Distance	Difference	Elevation
1		0	1.49	589.893
2		3.1	3.09	587.8447
3		5.7	3.07	587.8647
4		7.9	3.1	587.8347
5		8.7	2.04	588.8947

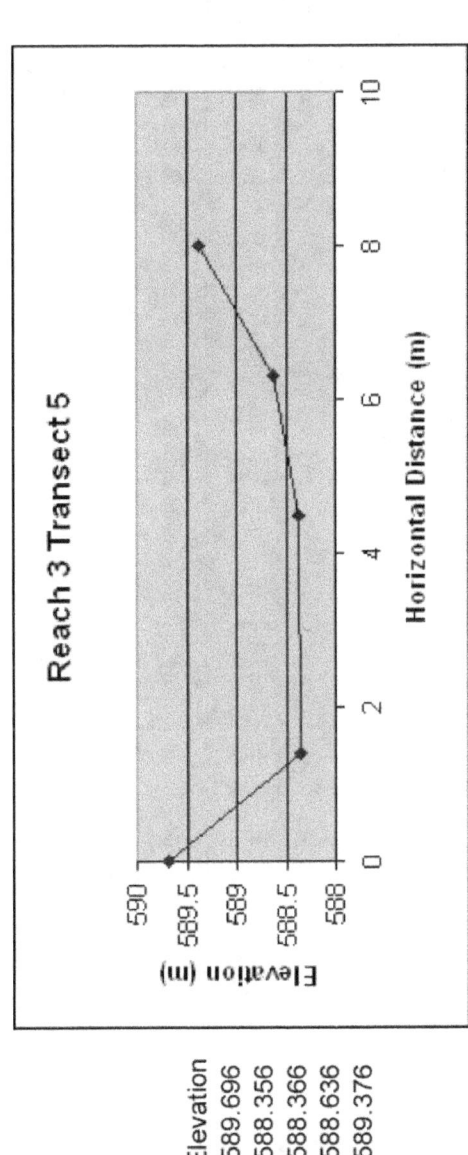

Reach 3 Transect 5

Transect 5   Looking downstream, right

GPS   Latitude   Longitude
       35° 37.270   99° 41.281

Point	Distance	Difference	Elevation
1	0	1.72	589.696
2	1.4	3.06	588.356
3	4.5	3.05	588.366
4	6.3	2.78	588.636
5	8	2.04	589.376

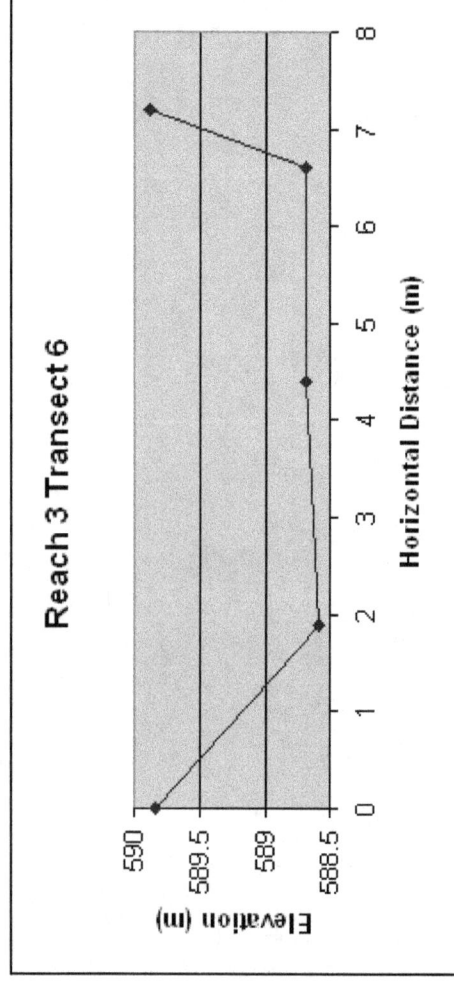

Reach 3 Transect 6

Transect 6	Looking downstream, right		
GPS	Latitude	Longitude	
	35°	99°	
	37.256	41.313	

Point	Distance	Difference	Elevation
1	0	1.885	589.842
2	1.9	3.14	588.587
3	4.4	3.04	588.687
4	6.6	3.04	588.687
5	7.2	1.84	589.887

Appendix A5. Cross-section profiles for 11 cross-sections in Reach #4 of WBNHS. Refer to Figure 3 and Table 2 for locations and substrate characteristics, respectively.

Transect 1   Looking downstream, left

GPS   Latitude   Longitude
             35° 37.460   99° 41.735

Point	Distance	Difference	Elevation
1	0	2.77	586.4315
2	2.1	3.59	585.6115
3	5	3.63	585.5715
4	8.2	3.63	585.5715
5	11.9	2.14	587.0615

Reach 4 Transect 1

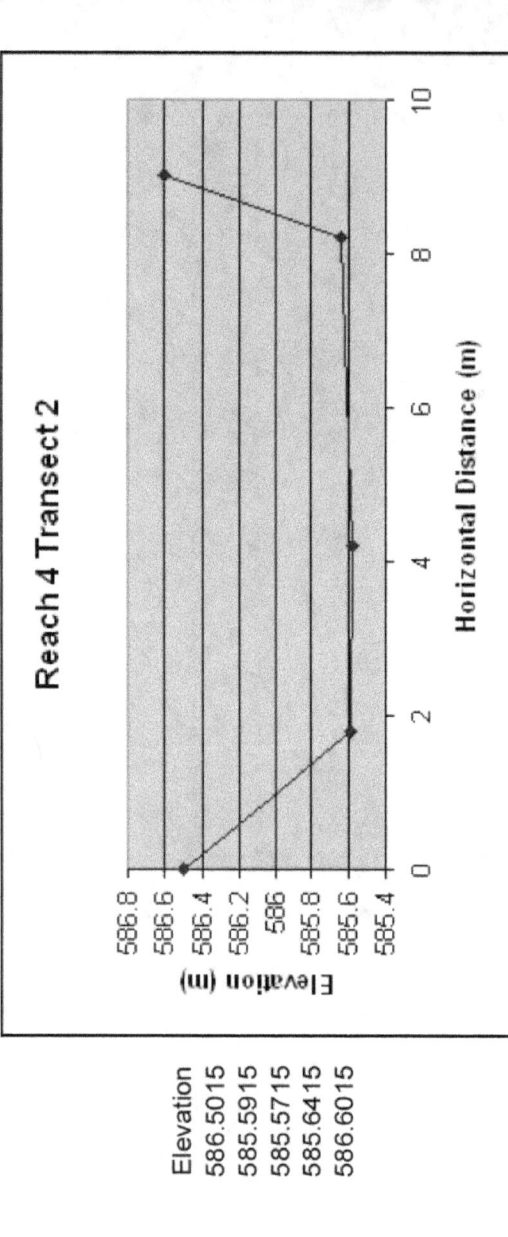

Reach 4 Transect 2

Transect 2

GPS   Looking downstream, left

Latitude   Longitude
35° 37.460   99° 41.765

Point	Distance	Difference	Elevation
1	0	2.7	586.5015
2	1.8	3.61	585.5915
3	4.2	3.63	585.5715
4	8.2	3.56	585.6415
5	9	2.6	586.6015

Reach 4 Transect 3

Transect 3

GPS   Looking downstream, left

	Latitude	Longitude		
	35° 37.477	99° 41.795		
Point	Distance	Difference		Elevation
1	0	1.63		587.1548
2	2.4	3.09		585.6948
3	4.75	3.13		585.6048
4	10.9	3.25		585.5248
5	12.9	1.94		586.8448

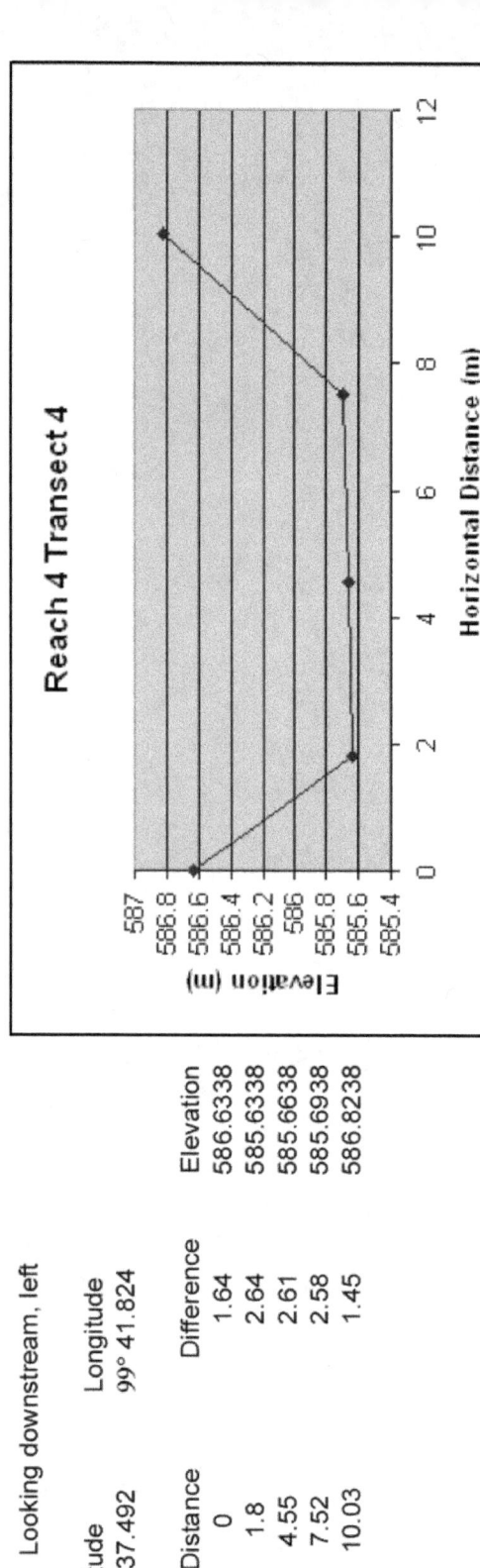

Reach 4 Transect 4

Transect 4				
GPS	Looking downstream, left			
	Latitude	Longitude		
	35° 37.492	99° 41.824		
Point	Distance	Difference	Elevation	
1	0	1.64	586.6338	
2	1.8	2.64	585.6338	
3	4.55	2.61	585.6638	
4	7.52	2.58	585.6938	
5	10.03	1.45	586.8238	

58

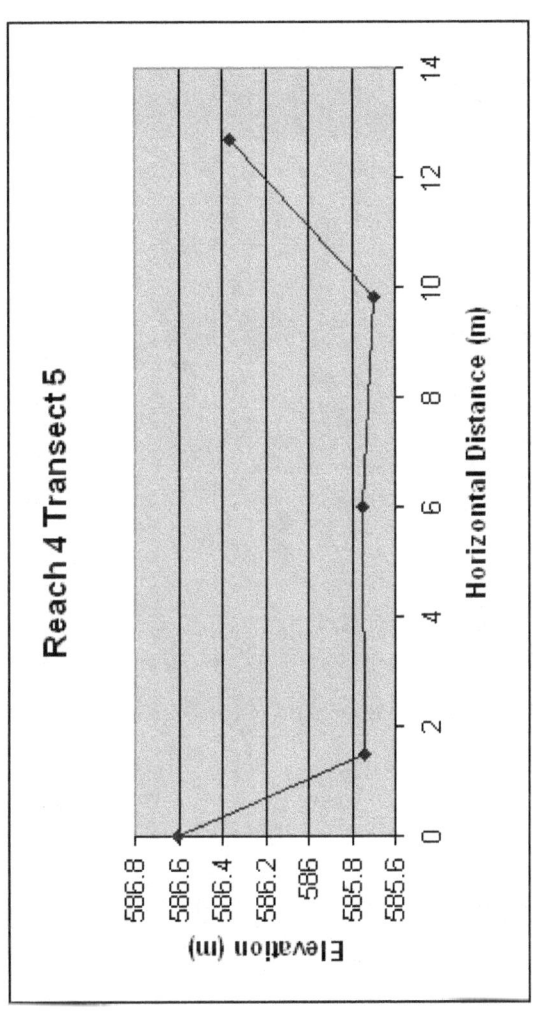

Reach 4 Transect 5

Transect 5   Looking downstream, left

GPS	Latitude	Longitude
	35°	99°
	37.501	41.852

Point	Distance	Difference	Elevation
1	0	2.68	586.6015
2	1.5	3.54	585.7415
3	6	3.53	585.7515
4	9.8	3.58	585.7015
5	12.7	2.92	586.3615

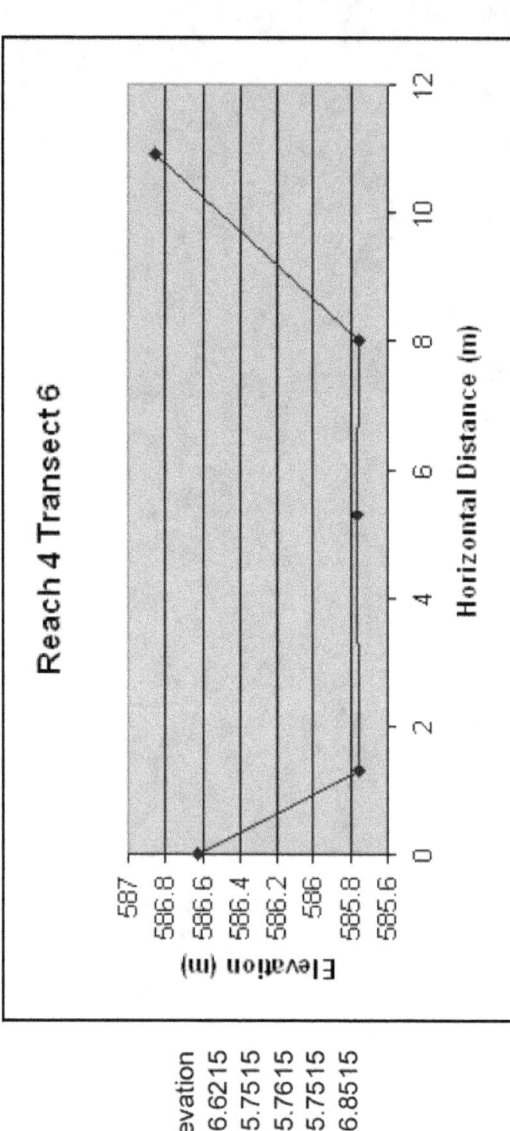

Reach 4 Transect 6

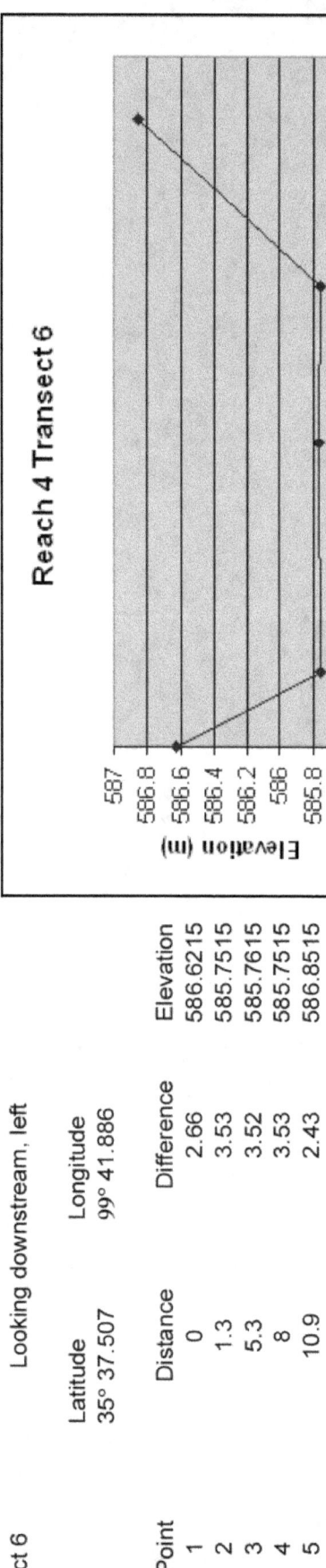

Transect 6

GPS

Looking downstream, left

	Latitude	Longitude	
	35° 37.507	99° 41.886	
Point	Distance	Difference	Elevation
1	0	2.66	586.6215
2	1.3	3.53	585.7515
3	5.3	3.52	585.7615
4	8	3.53	585.7515
5	10.9	2.43	586.8515

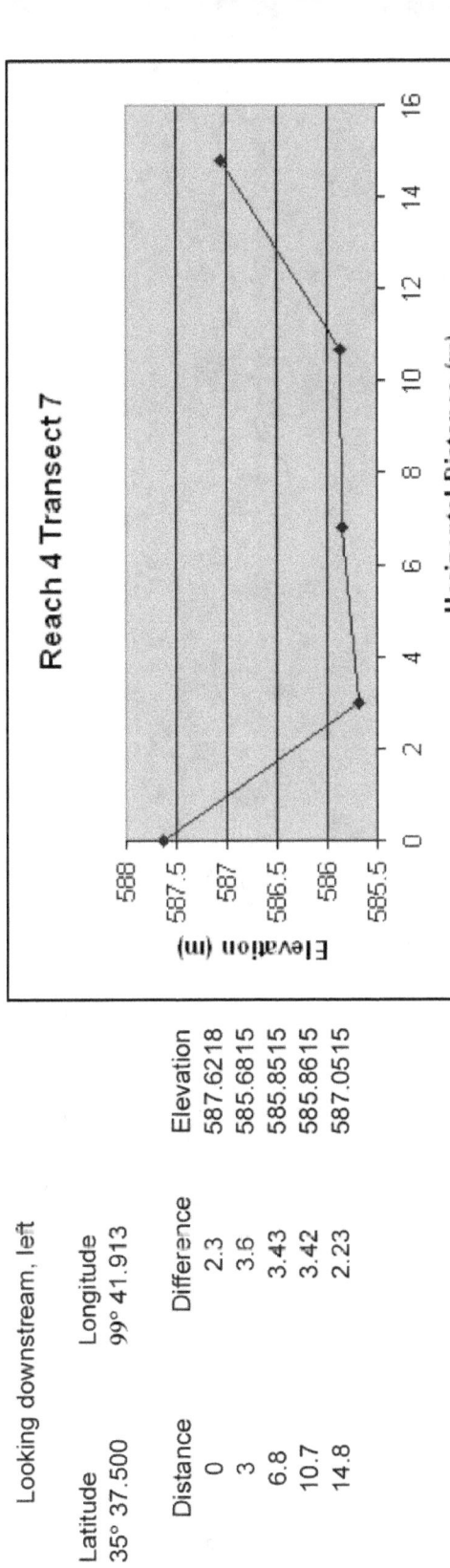

Reach 4 Transect 7

Transect 7   Looking downstream, left

GPS   Latitude   Longitude
       35° 37.500   99° 41.913

Point	Distance	Difference	Elevation
1	0	2.3	587.6218
2	3	3.6	585.6815
3	6.8	3.43	585.8515
4	10.7	3.42	585.8615
5	14.8	2.23	587.0515

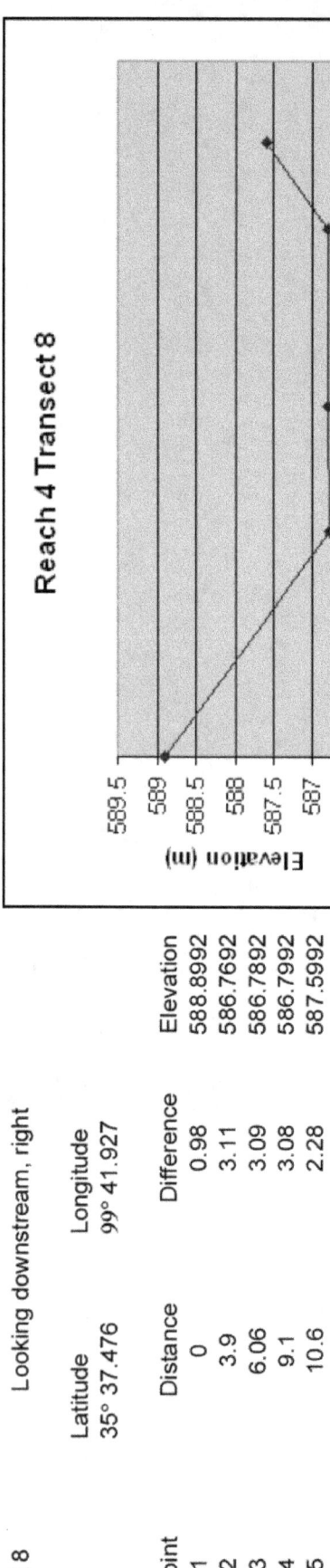

Reach 4 Transect 8

Transect 8

GPS   Looking downstream, right

	Latitude	Longitude		
	35° 37.476	99° 41.927		
Point	Distance	Difference	Elevation	
1	0	0.98	588.8992	
2	3.9	3.11	586.7692	
3	6.06	3.09	586.7892	
4	9.1	3.08	586.7992	
5	10.6	2.28	587.5992	

Transect 9   Looking downstream, right

GPS   Latitude   Longitude
             35° 37.466   99° 41.959

Point	Distance	Difference	Elevation
1	0	1.94	587.9392
2	1.6	3.01	586.8692
3	4.3	3.05	586.8292
4	7	3	586.8792
5	8.6	1.81	588.0692

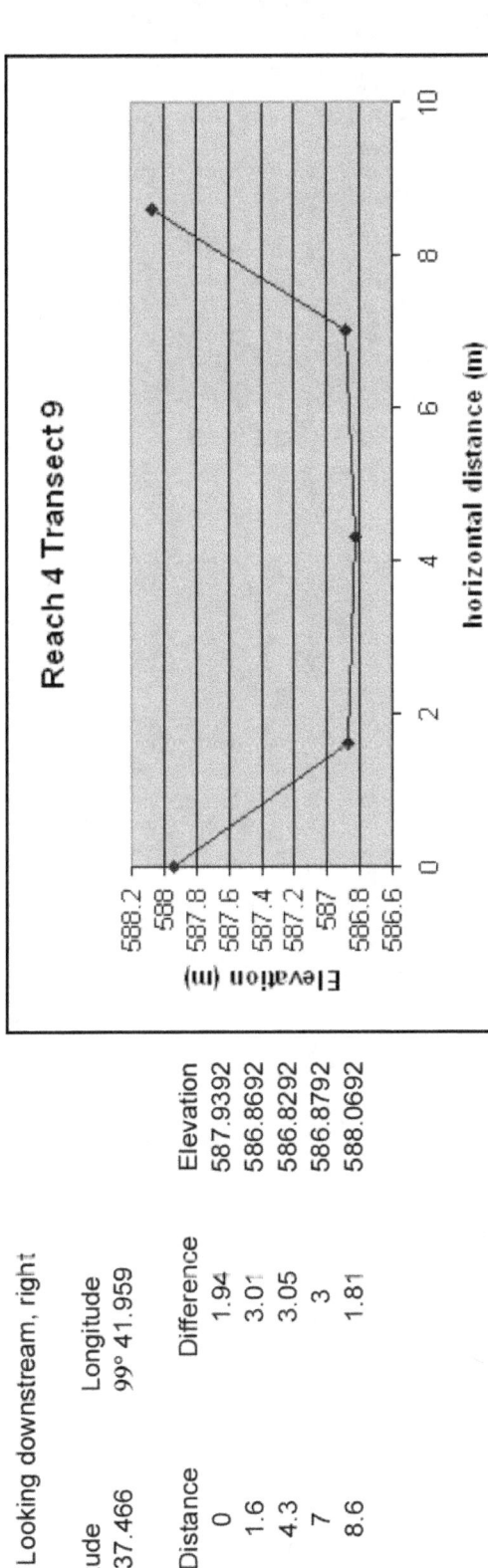

Reach 4 Transect 9

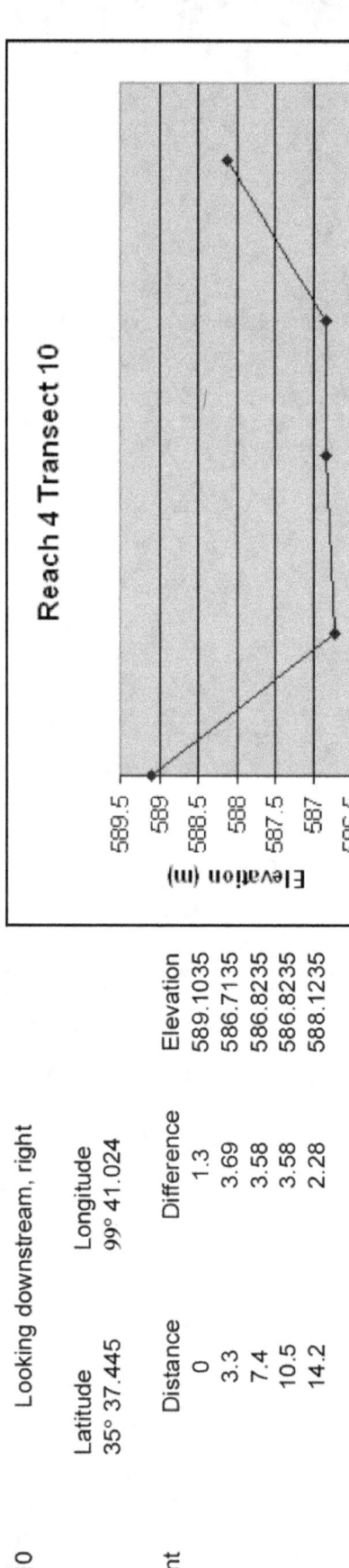

Reach 4 Transect 10

Transect 10

GPS   Looking downstream, right

	Latitude	Longitude
	35° 37.445	99° 41.024

Point	Distance	Difference	Elevation
1	0	1.3	589.1035
2	3.3	3.69	586.7135
3	7.4	3.58	586.8235
4	10.5	3.58	586.8235
5	14.2	2.28	588.1235

64

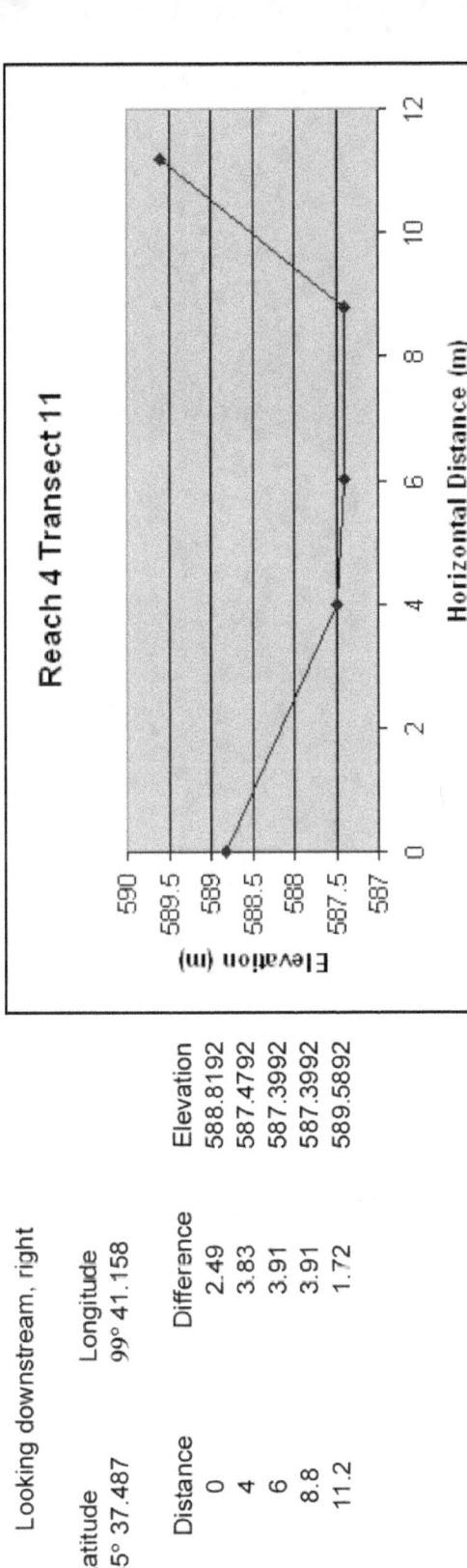

Reach 4 Transect 11

Transect 11				
GPS		Looking downstream, right		
	Latitude	Longitude		
	35° 37.487	99° 41.158		
	Point	Distance	Difference	Elevation
	1	0	2.49	588.8192
	2	4	3.83	587.4792
	3	6	3.91	587.3992
	4	8.8	3.91	587.3992
	5	11.2	1.72	589.5892

Appendix B: WATER LEVEL DATA
IN WELLS AT THE WBNHS

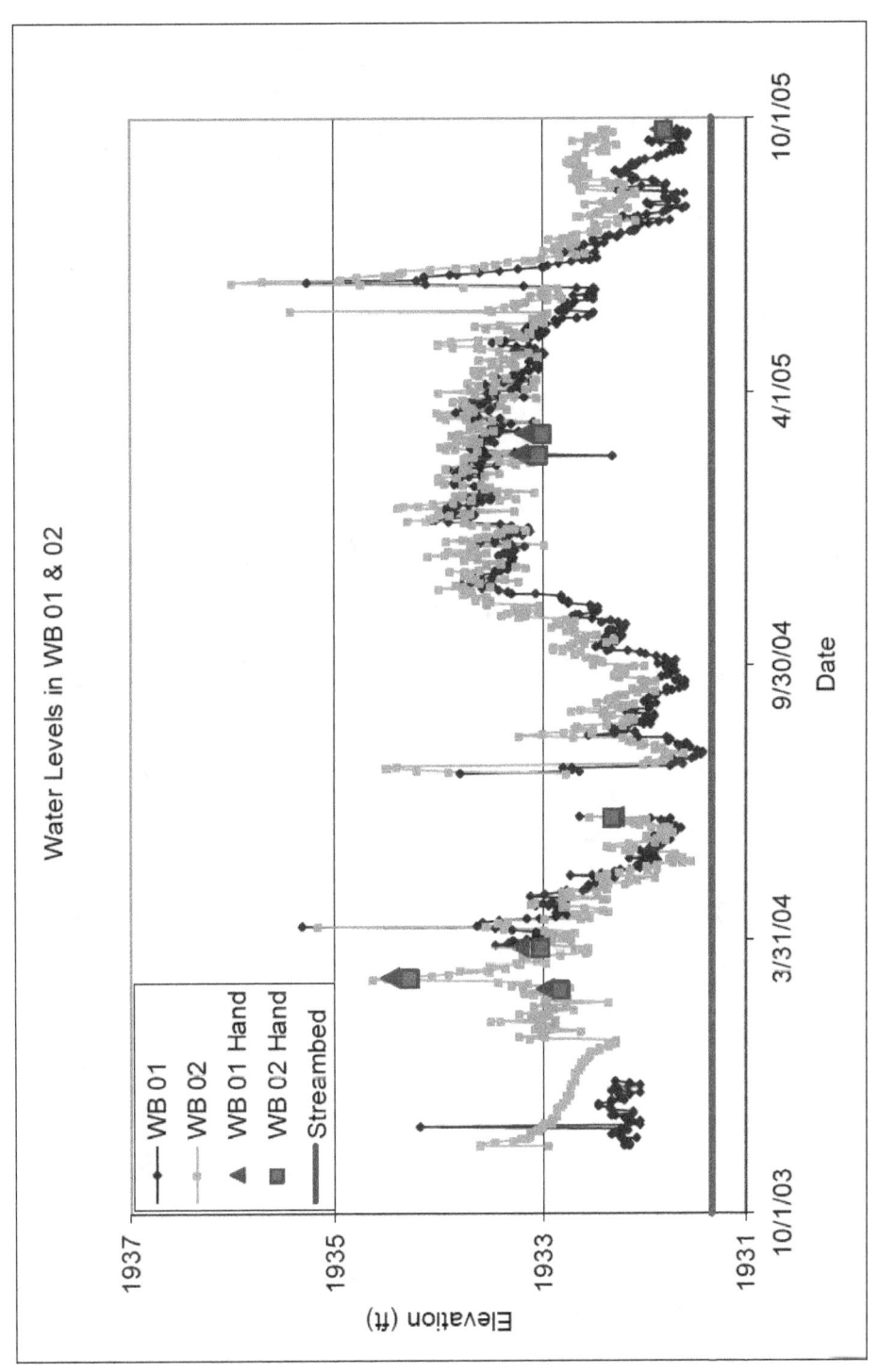

Figure B1. Water level data from monitoring Wells WB-01 and WB-02 on the western side of the WBNHS. Continuous lines represent transducer data collected continuously during the study period. Individual symbols represent hand measurements collected during sampling periods. Note that during the study period the elevation of the ground water never went below the elevation of the streambed.

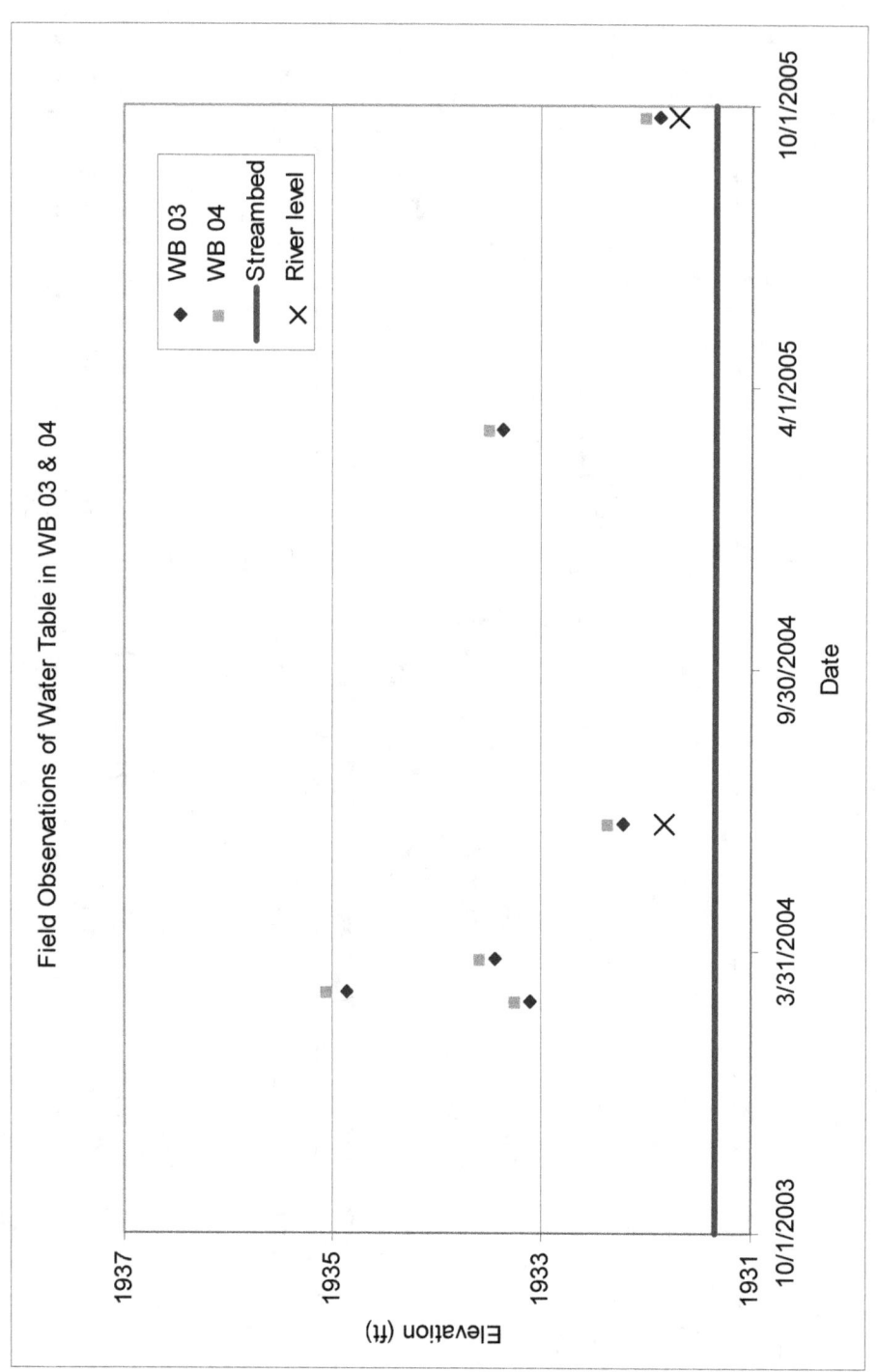

Figure B2. Water level data from monitoring Wells WB-03 and WB-04 on the western side of the WBNHS. No transducers were installed in these wells during the study period. Individual symbols represent hand measurements collected during sampling periods. Note that during the study period the elevation of the ground water never went below the elevation of the streambed or the level of the river.

70

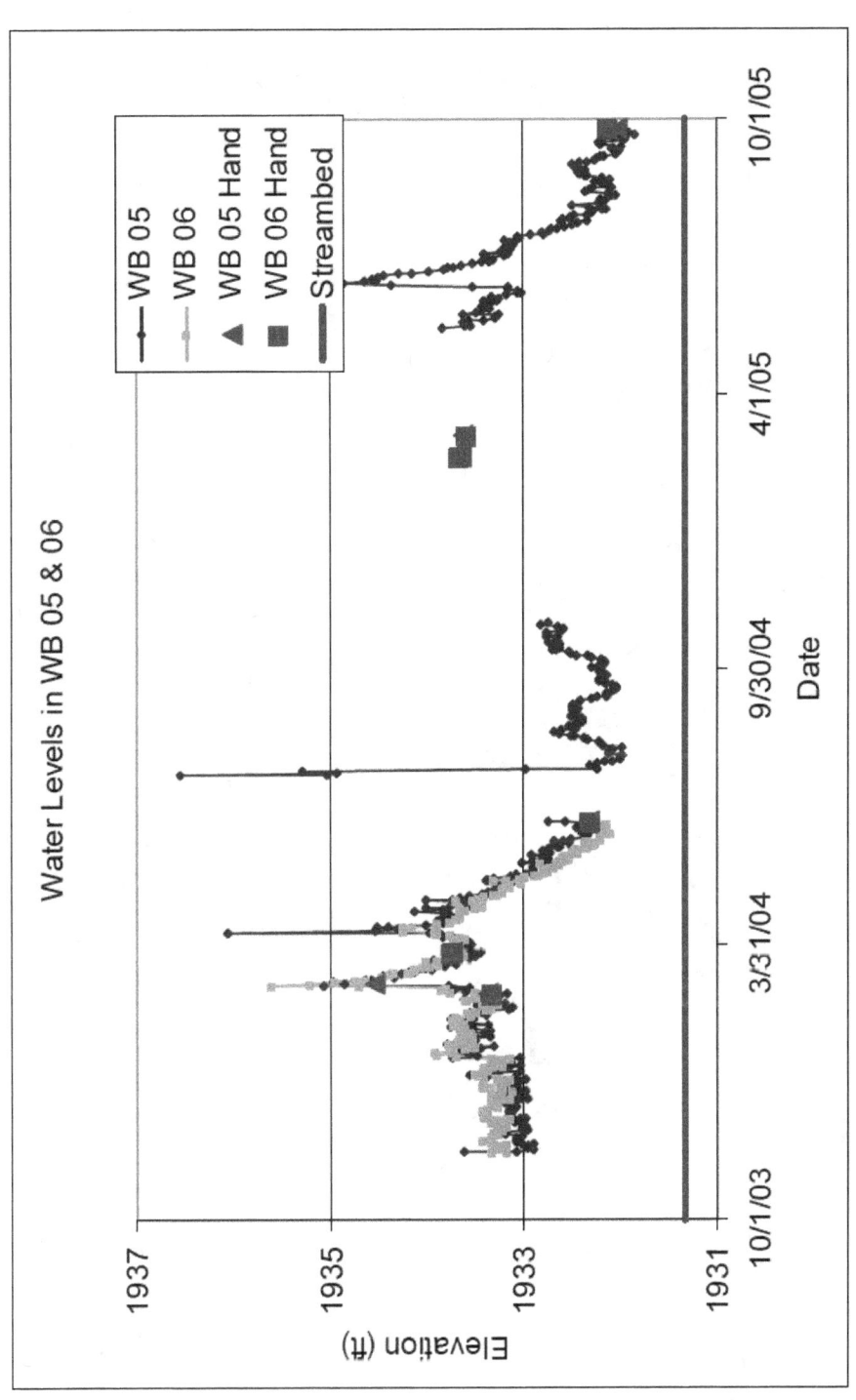

Figure B3. Water level data from monitoring Wells WB-05 and WB-06 on the western side of the WBNHS. Continuous lines represent transducer data collected continuously during the study period. Individual symbols represent hand measurements collected during sampling periods. Note that during the study period the elevation of the ground water never went below the elevation of the streambed.

71

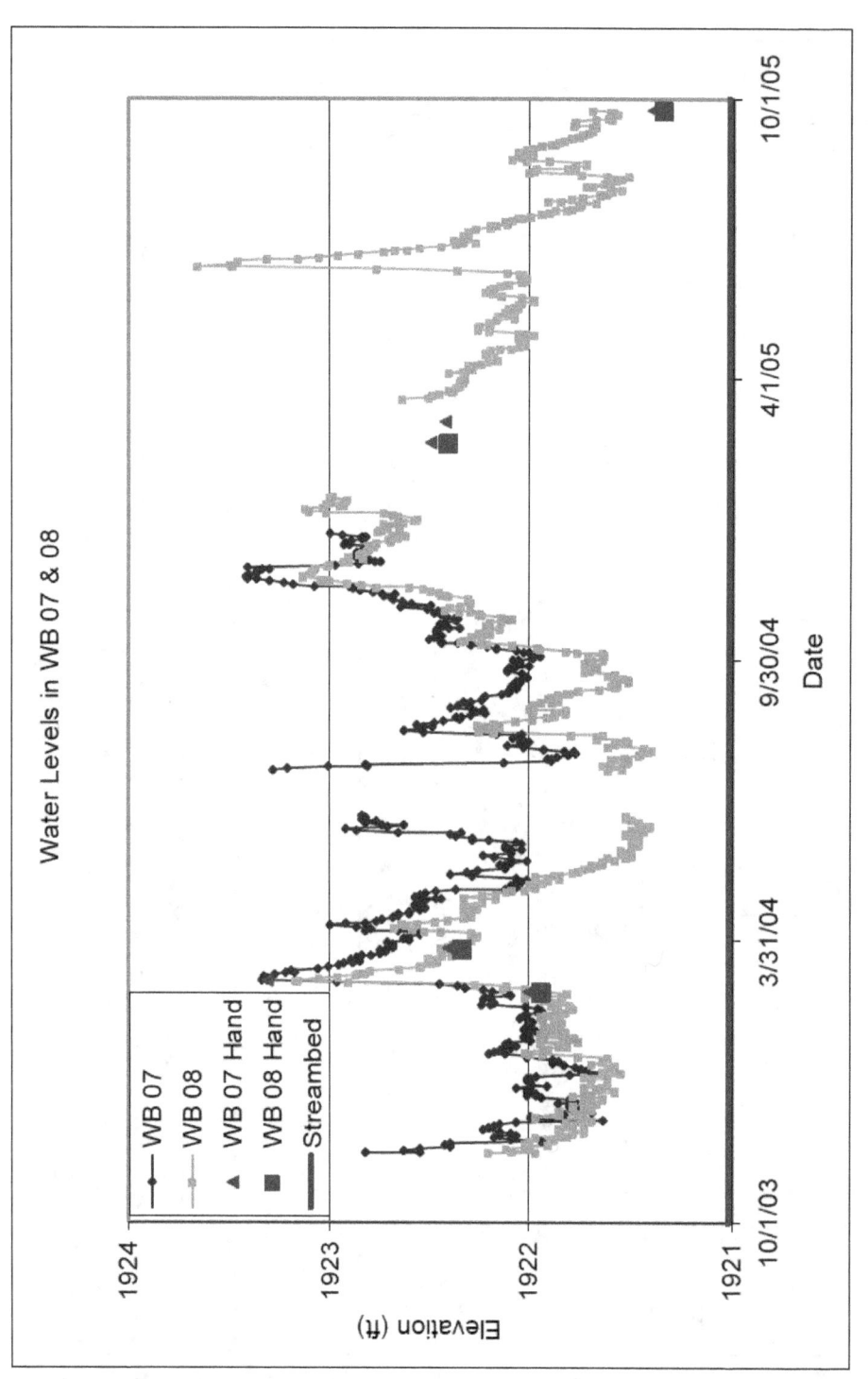

Figure B4. Water level data from monitoring Wells WB-07 and WB-08 on the eastern side of the WBNHS. Continuous lines represent transducer data collected continuously during the study period. Individual symbols represent hand measurements collected during sampling periods. Note that during the study period the elevation of the ground water never went below the elevation of the streambed.

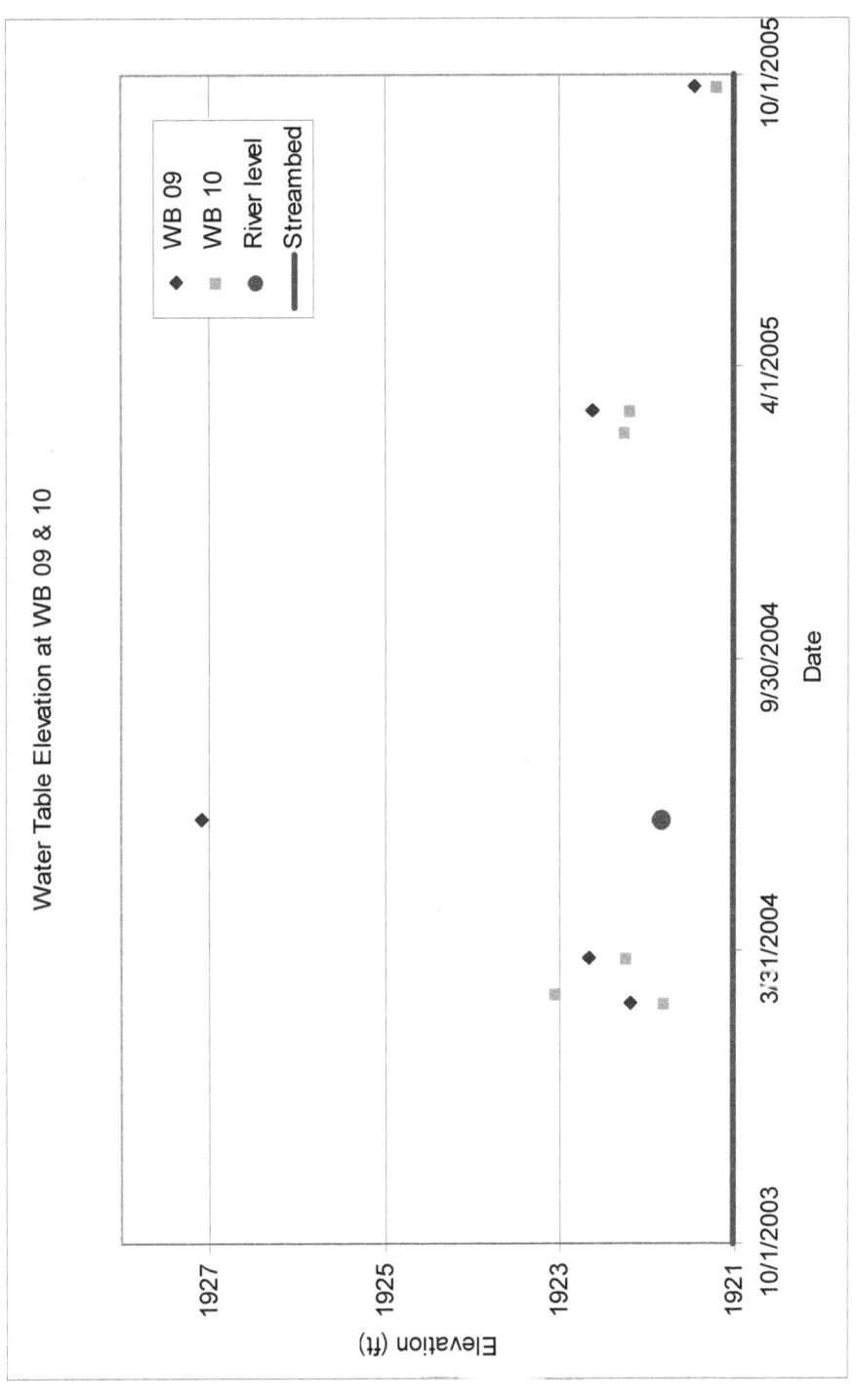

Figure B5. Water level data from monitoring Wells WB-09 and WB-10 on the western side of the WBNHS. No transducers were installed in these wells during the study period. Individual symbols represent hand measurements collected during sampling periods. Note that during the study period the elevation of the ground water never went below the elevation of the streambed or the level of the river.

APPENDIX C: ELECTRICAL RESISTIVITY
IMAGING (ERI) DATA AT THE WBNHS

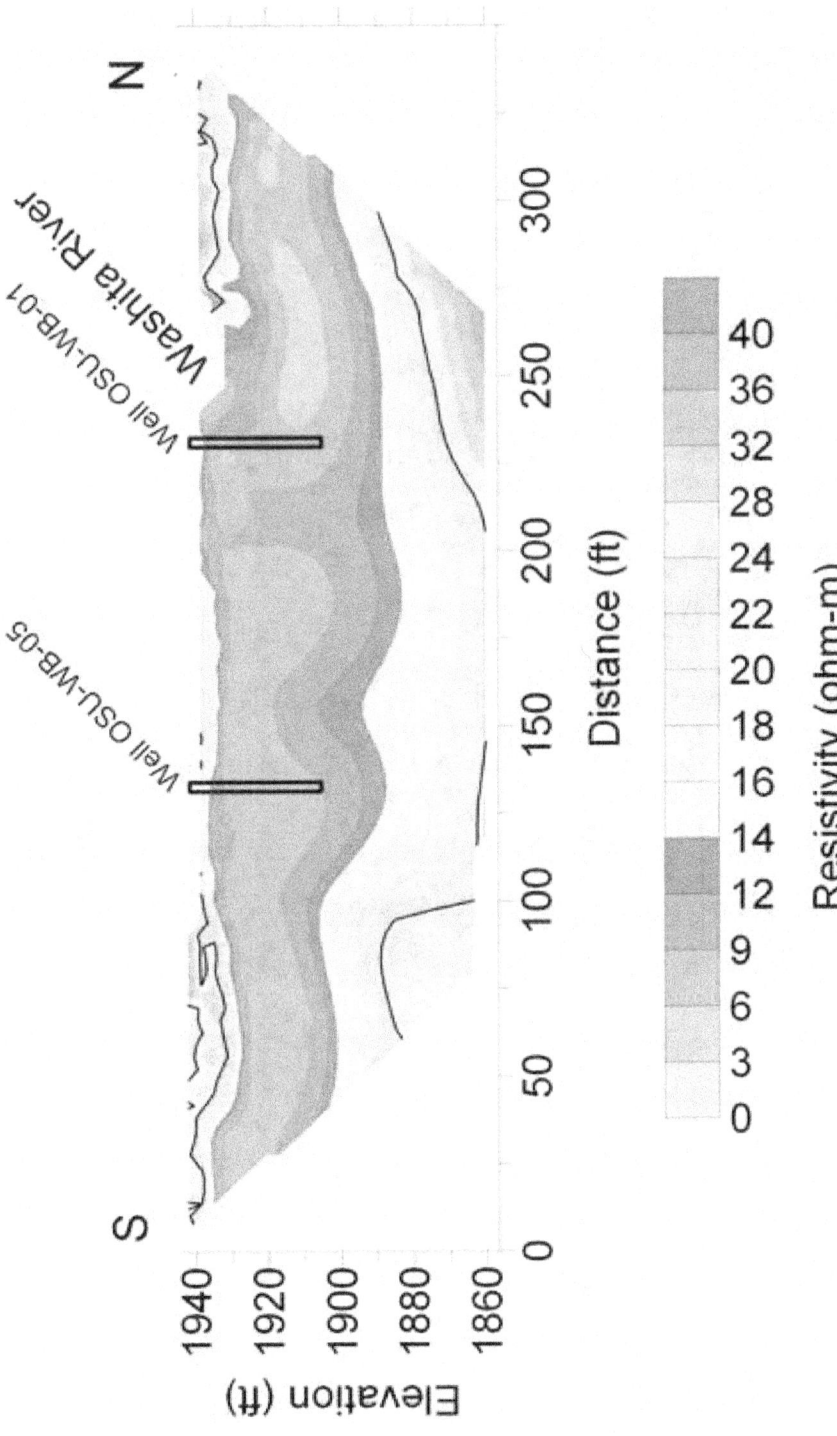

Figure C1. Electrical resistivity image (ERI) WB-12-04 collected through two well pairs on western edge of WBNHS during June 2004. The image has been calibrated with cooler colors equating to finer grain sediments. Warmer colors at the bottom of the image are likely bedrock.

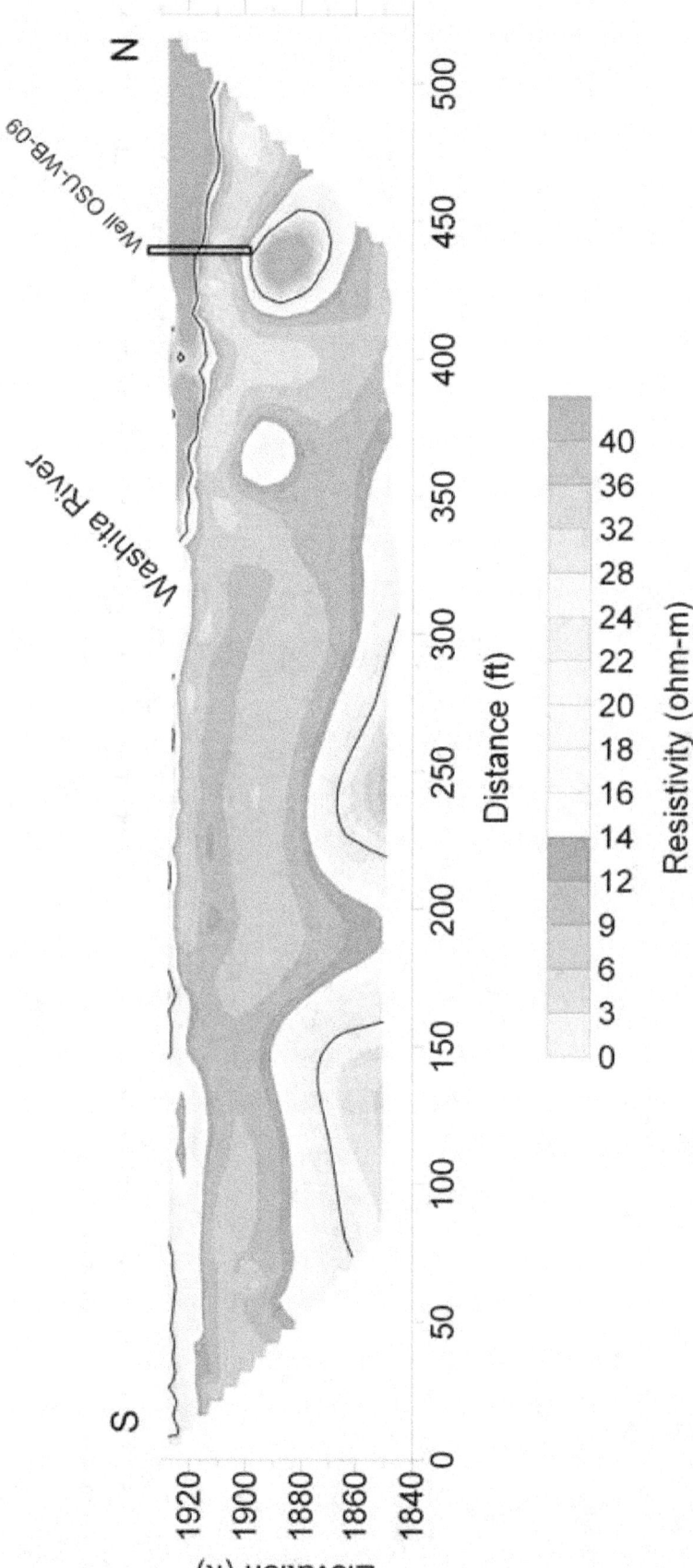

Figure C2. Electrical resistivity image (ERI) WB-36-04 collected through a well pairs on the eastern edge of WBNHS during June 2004. The image has been calibrated with cooler colors equating to finer grain sediments. Warmer colors at the bottom of the image are likely bedrock.

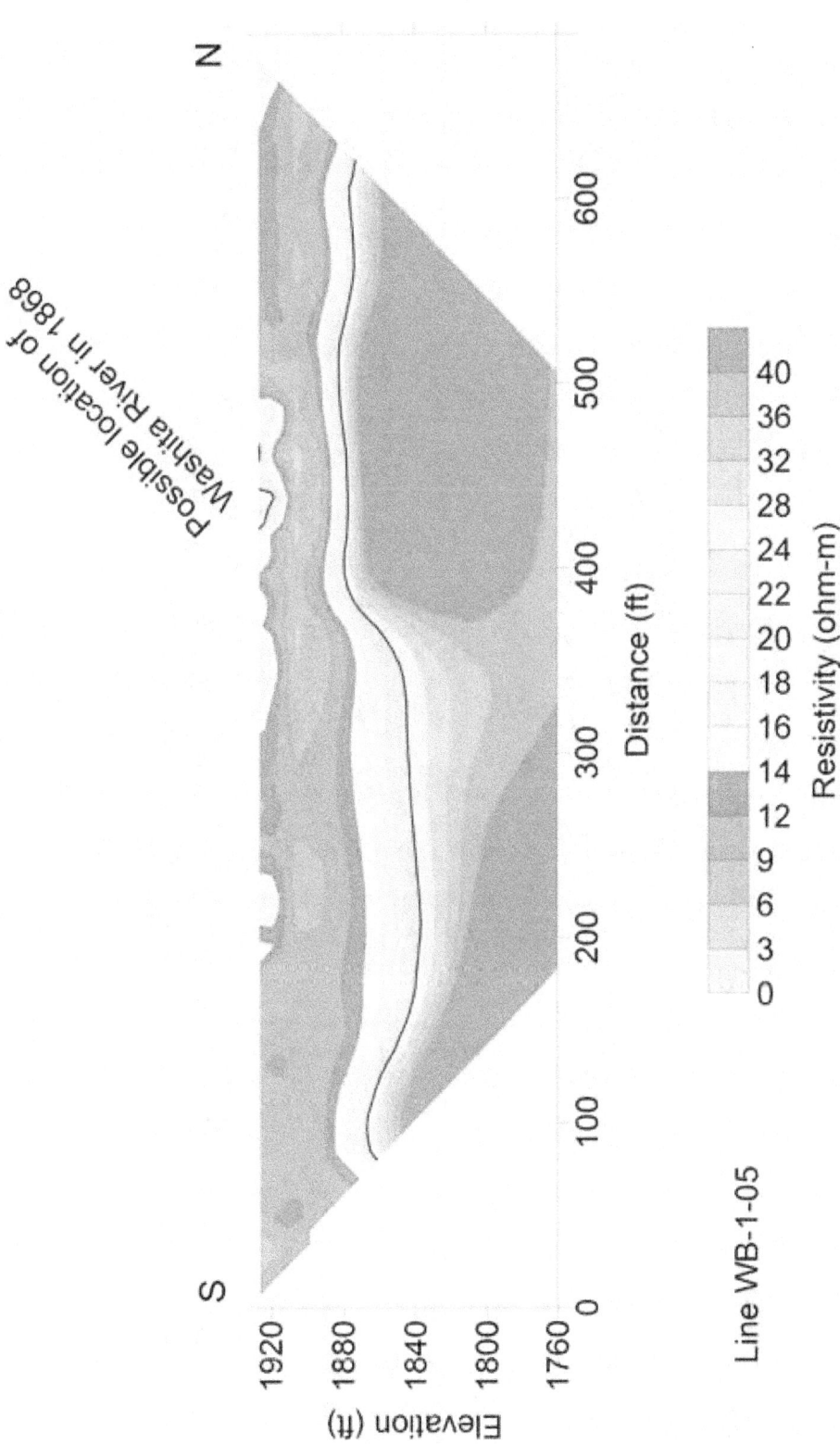

Figure C3. Electrical resistivity image (ERI) WB-1-05 collected through the potential location of the Washita River during 1868. Data were collected at WBNHS during May 2005. The image has been calibrated with cooler colors equating to finer grain sediments. Warmer colors at the bottom of the image are likely bedrock.

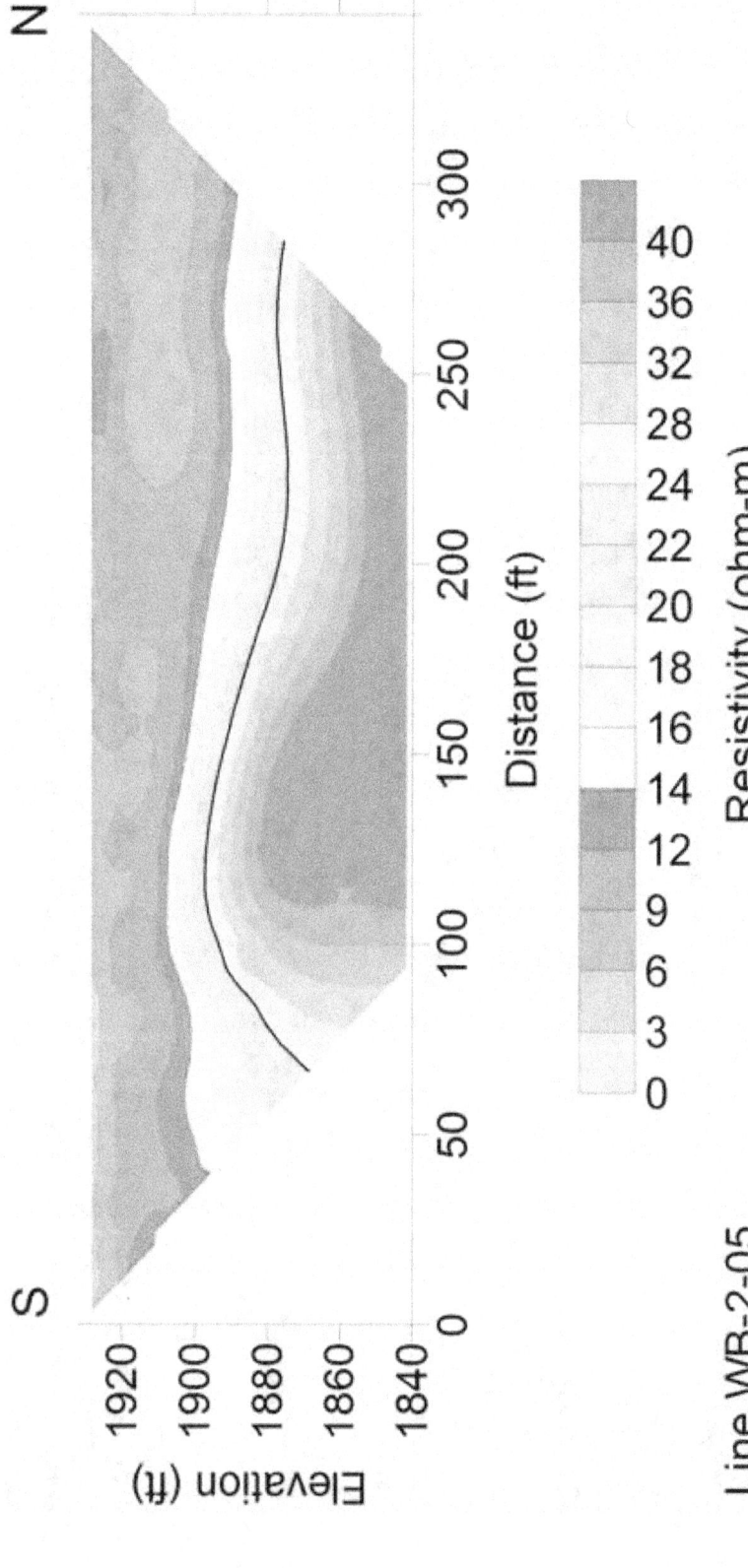

Line WB-2-05

Figure C4. Electrical resistivity image (ERI) WB-2-05 collected through the potential location of the Washita River during 1868. Data were collected at WBNHS during May 2005. The image has been calibrated with cooler colors equating to finer grain sediments. Warmer colors at the bottom of the image are likely bedrock.

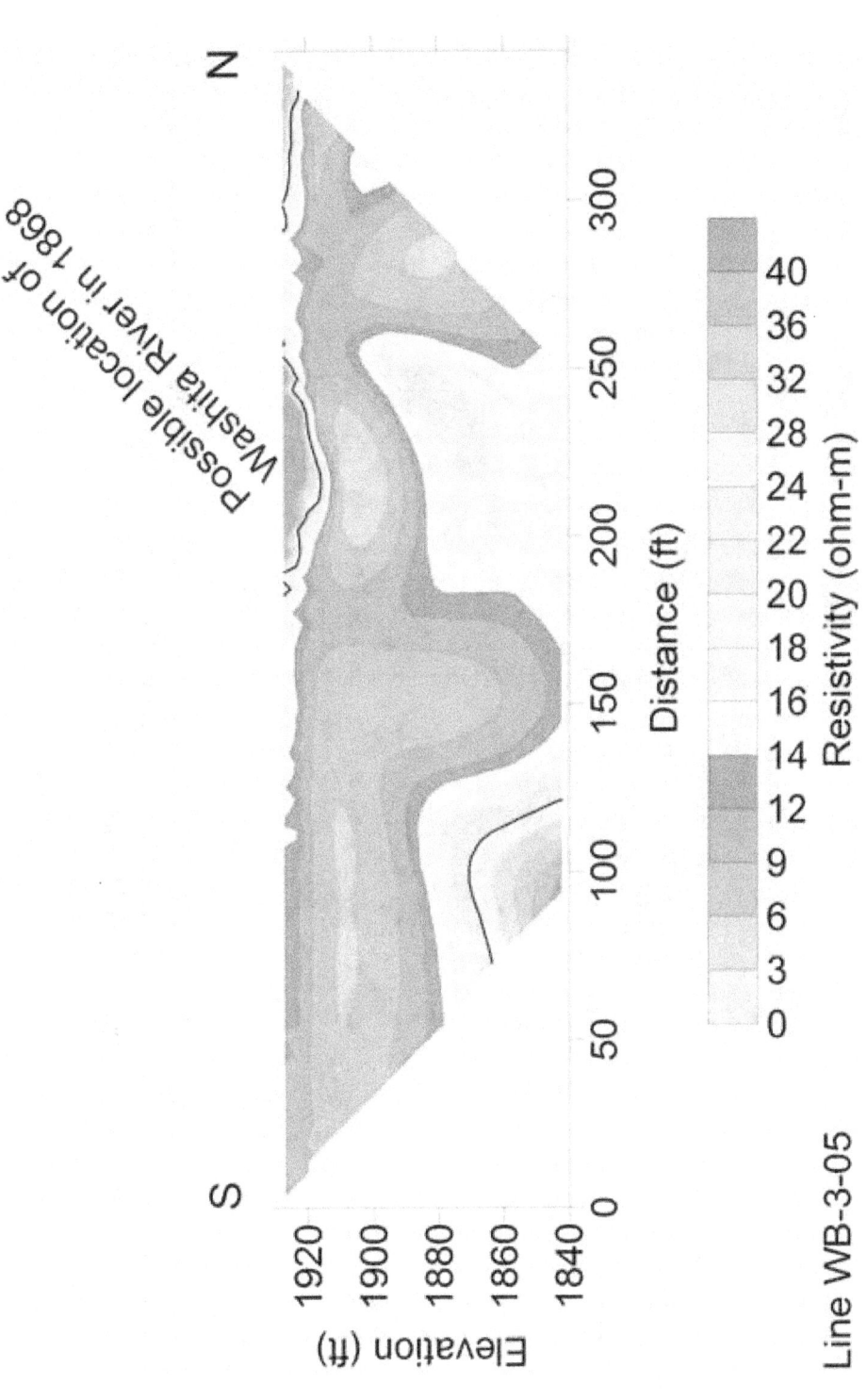

Figure C5. Electrical resistivity image (ERI) WB-3-05 collected through the potential location of the Washita River during 1868. Data were collected at WBNHS during May 2005. The image has been calibrated with cooler colors equating to finer grain sediments. Warmer colors at the bottom of the image are likely bedrock.

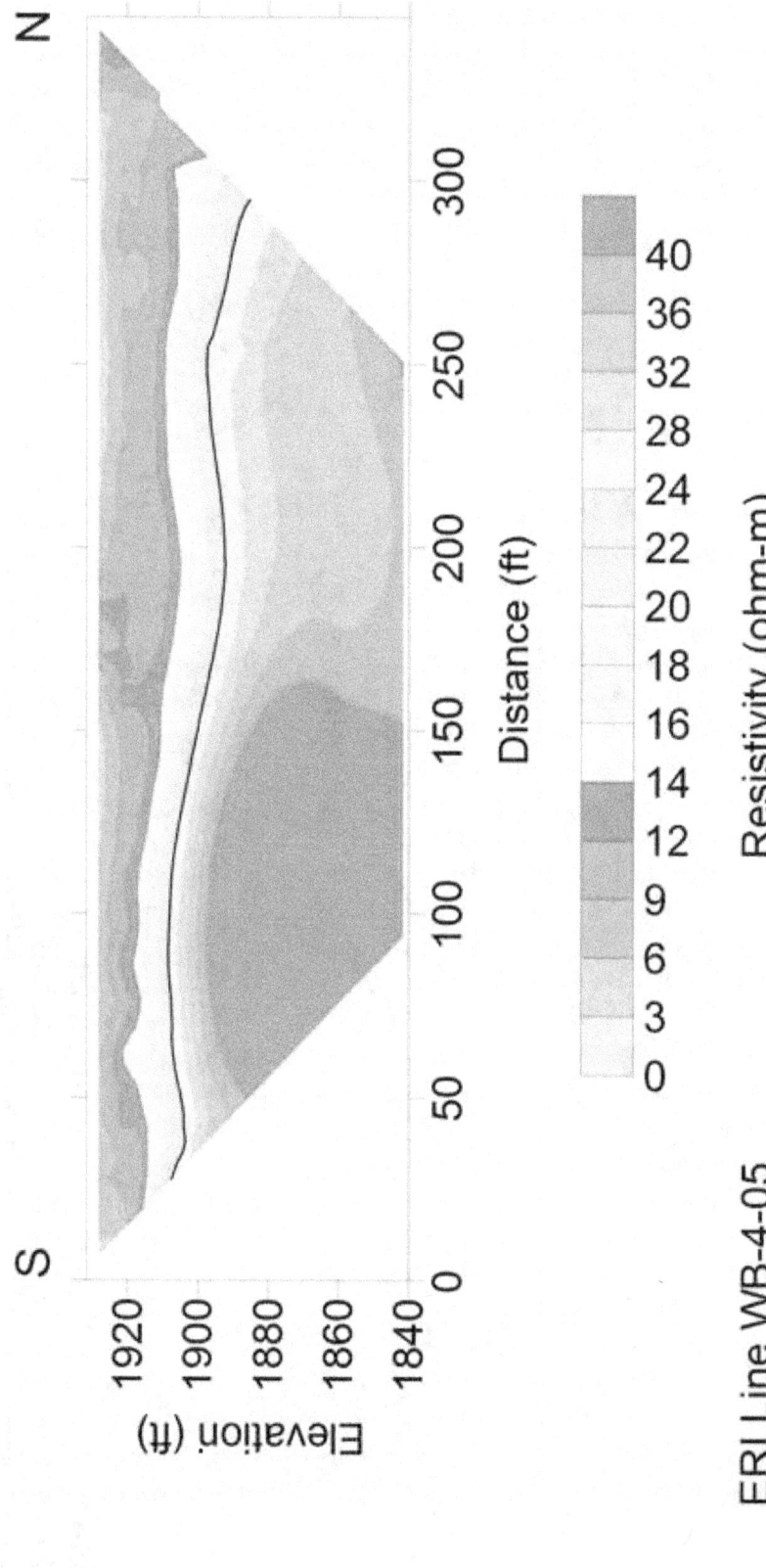

ERI Line WB-4-05

Resistivity (ohm-m)

Figure C6. Electrical resistivity image (ERI) WB-4-05 collected through the potential location of the Washita River during 1868. Data were collected at WBNHS during May 2005. The image has been calibrated with cooler colors equating to finer grain sediments. Warmer colors at the bottom of the image are likely bedrock.

82

NPS D-44A, December 2007